SUPERSTARS!™

JUSTIN BIEBER

The Story Continues...

SUPERSTARS!™

JUSTIN BIEBER

The Story Continues . . .

PRODUCED BY

DOWNTOWN
BOOKWORKS INC.

PRESIDENT Julie Merberg
SENIOR VICE PRESIDENT Patty Brown
EDITORIAL ASSISTANT Sara DiSalvo
EDITORIAL INTERN Emily Simon
SPECIAL THANKS Sarah Parvis, Claudia Atticot, Caroline Bronston

WRITER Sunny Blue
DESIGN Brian Michael Thomas/Our Hero Productions

Time
HOME ENTERTAINMENT

PUBLISHER Jim Childs
VICE PRESIDENT, BUSINESS DEVELOPMENT & STRATEGY Steven Sandonato
EXECUTIVE DIRECTOR MARKETING SERVICES Carol Pittard
EXECUTIVE DIRECTOR, RETAIL & SPECIAL SALES Tom Mifsud
EXECUTIVE PUBLISHING DIRECTOR Joy Butts
EDITORIAL DIRECTOR Stephen Koepp
EDITORIAL OPERATIONS DIRECTOR Michael Q. Bullerdick
DIRECTOR, BOOKAZINE DEVELOPMENT & MARKETING Laura Adam
FINANCE DIRECTOR Glenn Buonocore
ASSOCIATE PUBLISHING DIRECTOR Megan Pearlman
ASSISTANT GENERAL COUNSEL Helen Wan
ASSISTANT DIRECTOR, SPECIAL SALES Ilene Schreider
DESIGN & PREPRESS MANAGER Anne-Michelle Gallero
BRAND MANAGER, PRODUCT MARKETING Nina Fleishman
ASSOCIATE PREPRESS MANAGER Alex Voznesenskiy
ASSOCIATE PRODUCTION MANAGER Kimberly Marshall

SPECIAL THANKS Christine Austin, Jeremy Biloon, Stephanie Braga, Susan Chodakiewicz, Rose Cirrincione, Lauren Hall Clark, Jacqueline Fitzgerald, Christine Font, Jenna Goldberg, Hillary Hirsch, Suzanne Janso, David Kahn, Mona Li, Amy Mangus, Robert Marasco, Molly Martin, Robin Micheli, Amy Migliaccio, Nina Mistry, Dave Rozzelle, Adriana Tierno, Vanessa Wu

Published by Time Home Entertainment Inc.
135 West 50th Street • New York, NY 10020

ISBN 10: 1-60320-942-5
ISBN 13: 978-1-60320-942-7

We welcome your comments and suggestions about Time Home Entertainment Books. Please write to us at: Time Home Entertainment Books, Attention: Book Editors, P.O. Box 11016, Des Moines, IA 50336-1016

If you would like to order any of our hardcover Collector's Edition books, please call us at 1-800-327-6388, Monday through Friday, 7 a.m. to 8 p.m., or Saturday, 7 a.m. to 6 p.m., Central Time.

1 QGD 12

CONTENTS

ER

RB

SCHOOL
BOY

READ IT . . .
TO BELIEVE IT

Justin Drew Bieber of Stratford, Ontario . . .

Discovered on YouTube by a young American
talent manager named Scooter Braun . . .

Mentored by R&B superstar Usher and main man at
Island Records, L.A. Reid (*The X Factor*) . . .

Released debut single "One Time" in 2009 . . .

AND THAT WAS JUST THE BEGINNING . . .

WHY JUSTIN BELIEVES

from Prince of Pop to King of Swag

Justin has gotten street cred and plenty of props for his work up until now—his debut EP, *My World*, his first studio album, *My World 2.0*, his remix albums *My Worlds Acoustic* and *Never Say Never—The Remixes*, and his Christmas album, *Under The Mistletoe*. With these platinum-selling releases, Justin assumed the throne as the world's Prince of Pop, but his next album, *Believe*, has crowned him King. Justin's every song, every word, and every move are noted and quoted. We have watched him grow up from a talented 14-year-old newcomer to an 18-year-old icon. Today, he is one of the world's most influential performers, and its supreme ruler of swag.

"No one in the history of the world has ever grown up with the pressure that he has, being a solo artist that young, that famous, in a world with technology that exposes us 24-7," manager Scooter Braun said in a *Billboard* cover story. "He's a fighter. I'm proud of him—how he's stayed true to himself and [has] taken control of the entire situation."

Fun Times in London

While doing press promotion for his London concert, Justin surprised his interviewer at London's Capital FM radio: the Biebs did the whole interview with a British accent. Blimey! Using his accent, which he described as part Madonna, part Prince William, and part Robert Pattinson, the cheeky Canadian asked the reporter, "Do you think that my English accent's quite good, my friend? I think that if you walk in, you might not even know that I'm not an Englishman. I should just talk like this all the time, I think. It's quite. . . rubbish."

Surrounded by bodyguards, Justin is rushed through a London crowd of paparazzi and fans during his All Around The World Tour. He also debuted his new blond-ish hair!

"I don't want to lose my young fans, but I also want to mature and develop. I always keep one foot out of my comfort zone, trying new things and experimenting—if you don't, people will get bored. Seeing the smiles on people's faces and how I affect them when I perform makes me want to give them the absolute best experience they can possibly get." (*Billboard*)

Swaggy AND Social

"Your life is out there a lot more, especially nowadays when everybody has an HD camera phone on them at all times," Justin told *Billboard* about his worldwide fame. "My whole career launched from the internet, so without it, I feel like I wouldn't even be here. I owe a lot of my success to social media, to Twitter, to YouTube, and Facebook. It is also a great way to interact with fans."

And interact with his fans, he does. Justin's fans, or Beliebers, often discuss him and his music through views and comments on YouTube videos, Tweet responses, text alerts about Bieber sightings, ticket sales, music releases, and Facebook "likes" or "pokes." By July, Justin had more than 24 million Twitter followers, and his fans expect him to beat out Lady Gaga as the most-followed person on Twitter by the end of 2012.

His fans' expectations may be correct. Given that *Billboard* named Justin "Top Social Artist of 2012," the odds seem to be in Justin's favor.

Before going on stage at Wango Tango 2012, Justin tweeted his fans, "I heard 3 years ago today i did my first tweet. wild. alot has changed. thanks for growing with me and taking the journey. more to do."

"I'm 18 years old and I'm a swaggy adult! Come on, swaggy bros!" (GQ)

Swaggy as ever, Justin performs at the 2012 Billboard Music Awards in Las Vegas.

11

Wowing in white, Justin rocked the Billboard Music Awards with a high-energy, dance-driven version of "Boyfriend." The backup dancers busted out and the audience jumped to its feet with a thunderous ovation.

Thank You

"I just want to say how much of a blessing it's been the past three, four years, just growing up in front of everybody," Justin told the audience at the 2012 *Billboard* Music Awards after winning "Top Social Artist." "I want to thank all my fans, 'cause the internet is where I got my start. I want to thank my boy [and manager] Scooter Braun for all he's done. He's more than just a manager to me. I want to thank Usher.

. . . He takes the time to really care. I just want to say 'thank you so much' to my mom and my dad and to God. I could keep rambling forever. I just want to thank you so much. Swaggy."

That thank you wasn't the first time Justin has reached out to his fans to tell them how much they mean to him and how much he owes them. At his June 2012 concert in Mexico City, Justin taped a video just for his audience. In the video, he told the thousands of Beliebers in attendance, "When I get sick, when I get hurt, you guys are the first to write messages to me, and I feel a responsibility and I hope that I'm there for you guys as much as you were there for me."

Before giving a free concert for over 200,000 people in Zócalo Plaza in Mexico City, Justin was presented with a plaque for selling more than 500,000 copies of his CDs in Mexico.

"Turn to You"

From the very beginning of his rise to fame and fortune, Justin has given mega-credit to his mom, Pattie Mallette. Justin will never forget the sacrifices Pattie made for him as a single mom. A child of divorce, Justin was lucky enough to have the love and support of both his parents, Pattie and Jeremy, but it was his mom who was there 24-7, encouraging all his creative talents while she struggled to keep a roof over his head, feed, clothe, and educate him. It was Pattie who bought him his first drum set, and Pattie who put his first videos on YouTube. It was Pattie who guided him, looked out for him, and worried about him in his early professional days when they moved from Canada to Atlanta, Georgia. As Justin's stardom soars to almost unbelievable heights, he can always depend on his mom for her love and support.

What better way to express his thanks to her than through music. In early May, Bieber released his single, "Turn To You," on iTunes. "I wrote a song for my mom," Justin told MTV News. "I'm going to put it out on Mother's Day. . . .She had me at like the age I am now. [It's about] just the struggles she went through and how brave she was, and I think the world needed to know that."

It's no wonder Justin believes in Pattie, as she has always believed in him.

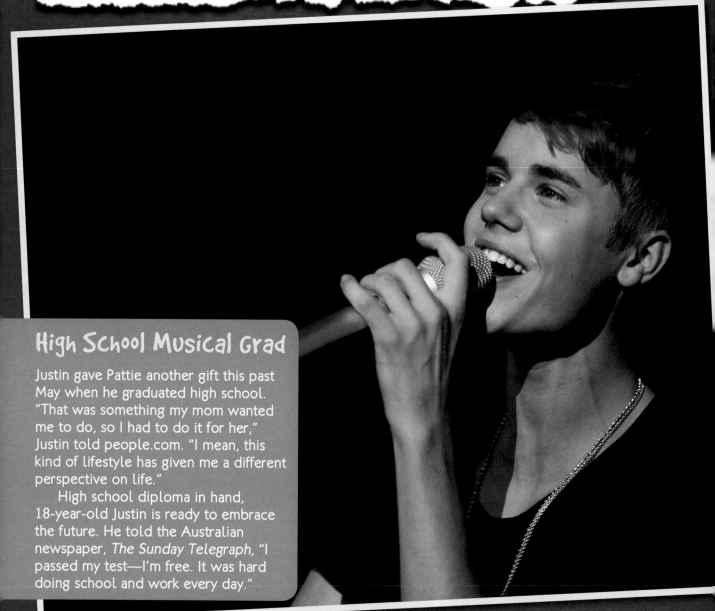

High School Musical Grad

Justin gave Pattie another gift this past May when he graduated high school. "That was something my mom wanted me to do, so I had to do it for her," Justin told people.com. "I mean, this kind of lifestyle has given me a different perspective on life."

High school diploma in hand, 18-year-old Justin is ready to embrace the future. He told the Australian newspaper, *The Sunday Telegraph*, "I passed my test—I'm free. It was hard doing school and work every day."

Justin is proud of his mom's upcoming memoir, *Nowhere But Up: The Story of Justin Bieber's Mom*. Due in September 2012, Pattie's memoir details the hardships and happy times on her journey with Justin.

"I'm proud of him. He's a really good kid, and he's headed in the right direction." (Scooter Braun on digitaljournal.com)

In the Public Eye

As probably the most recognizable teenager in the world, it's no surprise that wherever Justin goes, he's greeted by chants of "I Love You, Justin!" in one of many different languages. As he trots the globe, the singer is surrounded not only by frenzied fans, but also the ever-present press—whether it's the paparazzi's long-lensed cameras or such respected journalists as the *Today* show's Matt Lauer.

Justin admits that his fame can sometimes be overwhelming. If he wants to go to a movie at a local theater or shop at the mall with friends, well, it's almost impossible. If he doesn't attract a crowd of fans, he'll certainly have to dodge photographers trying to get their shot for a fan website or supermarket tabloid. He's grown to realize that this kind of attention comes with the level of success he's achieved.

Justin decided early on that he would use his position in the spotlight to make a greater impact. He has worked tirelessly as a spokesman for his favorite charity, Pencils of Promise, which helps educate children all over the world, builds schools, and encourages other kids to get involved. He also took part in a nationwide anti-bullying campaign when he lent his support to the film *Bully*.

A trailer for the film featured Justin singing the song "Born To Be Somebody," and he urged parents and kids alike to see the film. He's participated in other anti-bullying campaigns, such as television host Ellen DeGeneres' "Be Kind To One Another," which encourages bystanders to step in when they see someone being bullied.

A Good Heart

One Tree Hill star Sophia Bush has worked with Justin on several Pencils of Promise charity campaigns, and she was really impressed by his dedication and caring nature. "Bieber's doing a great thing," she told *OK!*. "He's a young superstar who could just be concerned with himself and his fabulous life. He is incredibly passionate about changing the lives of children around the world, and I think that is really commendable." She also told hollywoodlife.com, "For such a young kid, he has a really good head on his shoulders and I think it is a lovely thing to see someone who is so young . . . choosing to use his fame for good."

A Bieber Good Morning on *Today*

On June 15, 2012, thousands of Beliebers stormed the Big Apple. Justin was appearing on the *Today* show's Friday concert series, and fans from all over descended upon Rockefeller Plaza. It was reported that girls—many hailing from Georgia, Maine, California, and even Sweden—had camped out in the street for days just to score a place close to Justin and to prove they really did BELIEVE!

Justin's appearance on *Today* included an interview with host Matt Lauer. They discussed Justin's new album, *Believe,* and his hopes for making the transition from teen idol to accomplished musician. "I think [*Believe* is] about proving people wrong…going out there and making good music and… performing better than everyone else," Justin told Matt. "That's what I have to do to crossover [to being an adult performer], or else I'll just be another teen heartthrob, and I want to be remembered."

Justin discussed the good and the bad with Matt—including the fact that although he may be one of the world's top performers, he is still only human: "I'm 18 and I have a lot of insecurities," Justin admitted. "At the end of the day, being in my position doesn't get rid of those insecurities."

Maybe Justin should hear what his fans are saying. MTV News checked with them after the concert, and here are a few responses:

"The performance was amazing! We saw his face—his actual personal face. His new album is definitely his best. He sounds more mature."—Lacey

"My favorite part of the concert was when he sang 'Die In Your Arms,' because he just showed the romantic side of him."—Julieta

If his fans have anything to say about it, he'll slide right into full-fledged adult superstardom—they already think he's the man!

Justin wowed his fans singing songs from *Believe:* "Boyfriend," "All Around The World," and "As Long As You Love Me" as well as the classic, "Baby."

We're not sure why Justin's lifting his shirt, but we don't care, we just LOVE looking at his abs.

Justin was all smiles as fans sang along with his songs, chanted, "We want Justin!" and held up signs such as, "We just drove 14 hours. Why? Because we believe!" Another one , "My Buzz Lightyear Justin," which refers to his song, "Boyfriend," was his favorite sign!

Ever thankful to his fans, Justin made sure to take pictures with his Beliebers!

"I'm really excited to be able to travel the world again and see all my fans. Everyone, they got to believe," Justin told the crowd.

Justin's surprise guest for the *Today* show concert was Big Sean, who rapped along with him on "As Long As You Love Me." When they finished, Sean stepped up to the mic and said, "Make some noise for the legendary, one-and-only Justin Bieber." The crowd did just that, and Justin thanked his Beliebers with "I Love You!"

What's Next?

Over the past year Justin has grown up right before our eyes! Not only did he turn the magical age of 18 on March 1st, but he made his mark as a musical heavyweight when he won "Top Social Artist" at *Billboard's* Music Awards, "Fan Choice Award" at Canada's JUNO Awards, "UR Fave: Artist" and "International Video of the Year by a Canadian" for "Boyfriend" at Canada's MuchMusic Video Awards, and was dubbed Nickelodeon's Kids' Choice Awards "Favorite Male Singer"—all in the first six months of 2012. When his album, *Believe,* was released on June 19th, it rocketed to the top of the charts and sold 374,000 copies in the first week. Those were the biggest first-week sales numbers of the year . . . and of Justin's career!

Other moments on the boy-to-man Bieber journey have included appearing on the iconic *Saturday Night Live,* signing fellow Canadian artist Carly Rae Jepsen to his and manager Scooter Braun's record label, School Boy Records, introducing his second fragrance, Girlfriend, being featured in a two-night NBC documentary, *Justin Bieber: All Around The World,* and preparing to kick off his North American *Believe* tour in Arizona on September 29th. The tour will last through January 2013, when Justin will jet off to the rest of the world. Oh, BTW, Justin sold out his November 28th and 29th concerts at NYC's Madison Square Garden in 30 seconds!

Whew! It looks as if he's conquered the world already . . . so what could JB possibly dream up next? It seems that if he believes it, he can do it!

Justin excites London fans while in town for an All Around The World Tour concert in April 2012.

Big Screen Dreams

When Justin appeared as the troubled teen, Jason McCann, on TV's *CSI,* he got his first taste of drama in front of a camera. Now there is talk about Justin co-starring with Mark Wahlberg in an upcoming basketball-themed movie. "We're just waiting for the script," Wahlberg told Yahoo OMG!. "I've seen 115 pages of it and it's really good. It's kind of like *The Color of Money,* [first you had] Paul Newman and Tom Cruise, and now me and Justin Bieber. It could be very good."

It might also be a lot of fun behind the scenes if Justin and Mark start spitting out some raps. Justin has certainly earned his hip-hop creds, but what may be less well-known is that Mark first appeared on the show-biz scene as a rapper! He was the lead of Marky Mark and the Funky Bunch back in the 1990s, and their single "Good Vibrations" was a major hit—ch-check it out!

JUSTIN ON STAGE

All Around the World

In May 2012, Justin shot off a cryptic tweet—"ok. Going to board. OFF TO EUROPE! PHASE 1 of operation secret concerts! Lol. OSLO first stop. See u soon." And later, from the plane, Justin tweeted, "When I land [in Europe] #DieInYourArms and #BOYFRIEND will be out!! Countdown and then #BIEBERBLAST!!! Thanks! See u soon. Much love. #BELIEVE."

Justin's tweets were his first hints that he would give a series of free concerts in seven countries. Oslo, Norway was the first stop on this whirlwind trip, and the entire adventure was being filmed for an NBC documentary, *Justin Bieber: Around The World*, which aired in June 2012.

The journey generated plenty of Belieber-worthy headlines and images. Thousands more fans than expected turned out for his concerts, requiring last-minute extra security. At Justin's London show he did a little striptease for the crowd, showing off his abs; and his mentor, Usher, made an appearance. Later in London, Justin turned heads boarding the bus for Germany in a bright blue jumpsuit. Justin sang "Boyfriend" to fans in Paris on a balcony—but backstage at a performance in the same city on a hotel rooftop, he ran into a glass wall as he was going off stage. Oops!

As Justin explained to TMZ, "There's a glass wall behind me, but there's a railing behind the glass. And so I went to reach for the railing and I hit my head on the glass. And I guess me and glass windows don't really go together." Though he was dazed, he returned to the stage to finish his act, but when he walked back to his dressing room, he passed out for about 15 seconds. Turned out he had a concussion!

Of course, Justin wasn't finished—later on, according to MTV News, he tweeted, "I will see u again Glass. I will have my revenge. BIEBER vs. GLASS. MGM LAS VEGAS 2013. Lol. #GottaLaughAtYourself."

Justin—always the jokester! Keep reading to follow him on his mini-tour and to see how he impressed Beliebers along the way.

The Voice on THE VOICE

In May Justin debuted his single "Boyfriend" on the singing competition show *The Voice*, and gave fans a taste of his upcoming *All Around The World* and *Believe* tours.

Justin is interviewed for Spanish television in Madrid.

First Stop: Oslo, Norway

The Oslo Opera House, home of The Norwegian National Opera and Ballet, is one of Norway's most prestigious performance centers. And on May 30, 2012, it was the place to be if you were a true-blue Belieber! But security had such difficulty controlling fans that the police almost had to shut down the outdoor show. According to TMZ, Justin stepped in and tweeted, "Norway—please listen to the police. I don't want anyone getting hurt. I want everything to go to plan but your safety must come first . . . for the show to happen u must all listen to the police."

When things finally settled down, he tweeted again—"and tonight we will have some fun. love you and im excited to see you all. NORWAY...THANK YOU FOR HAVING ME! #BELIEVE"

On Tour Fun Facts

➜ Justin requested Union Jack seat cushions for his dressing room chairs when he performed at London's Wembley Stadium. (people.co.uk)

➜ After his run-in with the glass wall in Paris, Justin thought his eyebrow was paralyzed! "I can't move my eyebrow," he said in a video. But not to worry, all was well by the end of the day! (viddy.com video)

➜ In an interview with the *Today* show's Matt Lauer, Justin took the heat for losing the Superstar-Glass Wall matchup: "I'm pretty clumsy and I don't see glass walls. I think I wasn't wired to see glass walls. . . . I'm all right. I've had concussions, I used to play hockey."

➜ While in London, U.K. TV host and producer Alan Carr challenged Justin to a soccer match. Guess what? Our boy won!

➜ One of Justin's pre-show chants with his team is, "ducks, ducks, ducks, ducks, quack, quack, quack, quack," which is from the movie, *The Mighty Ducks*.

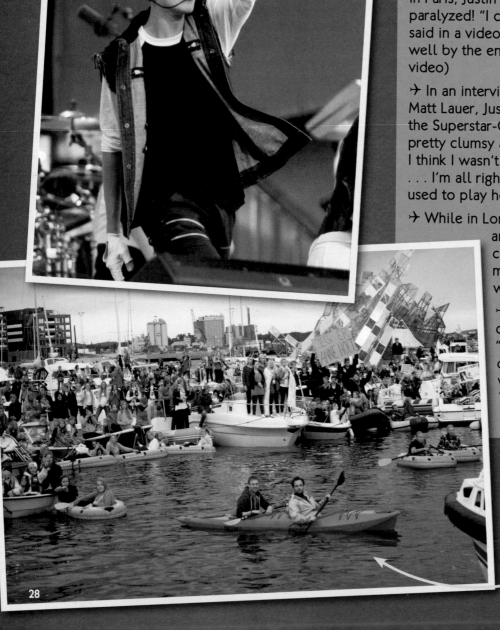

Fan Flotilla! Beliebers waited for hours in the Oslo harbor, aboard sailboats, yachts, kayaks, and a dinghy or two to hear the Biebs perform at the Oslo Opera House.

Justin had most of his [ ],000 fans singing along with him in Oslo. Though the concert got off to a bumpy start, the superstar finished it with a resounding "THANK YOU!" and was ready to take on the rest of his nonstop mini-tour!

them, Justin performed an acoustic set that included the songs, "All Around The World," "As Long As You Love Me," "Turn To You," "Die In Your Arms," and "Boyfriend."

The Gentleman of Verona... and Milan!

Justin spent June 2, 2012 in Italy—but he had no time to be a tourist. His schedule didn't allow for seeing the historic sites or lingering at cafés to sip espresso. He had to make two stops in the cities of Milan and Verona. First, in Milan, Justin did all the pre-show rituals—interviews, meet-and-greets, and warm-ups. Before he hit the stage at the Discoteca Alcatraz Milano, Justin tweeted, "Interviews done! About to perform for my fans in Milan. Good food. Good people. Love you Italy!" Well, at least he had time to sample the famous Italian cuisine—a boy's gotta eat!

At the end of the show, Justin touched his heart, thanked the crowd, left the stage and tweeted, "Great show! Milan you were awesome. Off to Verona like my boy Romeo. Where's my Juliet? #Boyfriend #Believe." Only hours later Justin was on the stage of Arena di Verona. He performed his new single "Boyfriend," and it was taped for the hit Italian TV show *Lo Spettacolo Sta Per Iniziare*.

Before he finished his Italian sojurn, Justin tweeted one more time—"Thank you for a great day Italy! Headed to Spain #withdankanter."

After a romantic acoustic set in Milan, Justin took to the Arena di Verona stage like dynamite! The high-energy performance left the Italians wanting more, more, more! And what did Justin like most about his day in Italy? The people, of course! He tweeted that they were "so smiley." Who could blame them?

Bieber captures Berlin

On his first day in Germany on June 7th, Justin lived what most other teenage boys can only dream of: He spent the day with super model Heidi Klum. Justin's guest appearance on the season finale of *Germany's Next Top Model* included a performance of his single, "Boyfriend," as well as time to hang and joke around with Heidi, the show's host. According to a1social.com, Justin also took the time to encourage the *Top Model* contestants and tweeted, "Lots of beautiful ladies running the hallways at *Germany's Next Top Model*. You're all winners in my eyes."

The next day, Justin had some rare free time and was able to leave his hotel, The Ritz Carlton on Potsdamer Platz Square, to stroll around the city a bit. Dressed for the day, Justin was in an oversized sweater, black jeans, sneakers, and sunglasses, with a backpack slung over his shoulder. Aside from the bodyguards surrounding him, Justin looked like any other normal teen. Even though it was his day off, he stopped to sign autographs and chat with fans. After his walk, Justin tweeted, "my German fans have been singing for me all morning. About to head over to the BILD to return the favor. But first—lunch." His next stop was *BILD* magazine for an interview and an exclusive performance.

When it was time to leave Germany, Justin tweeted once more, "Great time in Germany. Can't wait to see you all again on the #BelieveTour next year!"

Justin won a lot of "girlfriends" when he and and Dan Kanter, his musical director and guitarist, performed an acoustic version of "Boyfriend" at the BILD offices!

Justin and his crew were asked to perform for the season finale of *Germany's Next Top Model*, and they turned it up for Heidi and the beautiful contestants.

Asked to share his thoughts about all the fans camping out in Mexico City hoping to get into his show, at first Justin said, "There is no one I admire so much to do something crazy." But then he admitted, "If Michael Jackson were here, I would do it for him. So I do understand the emotion the girls feel and that makes me feel very honored."

Viva Mexico!

June 11—the whole of Mexico City was on alert. Justin Bieber was coming to town! Beliebers had been camping out for days near the scheduled concert site, the Zócalo, which is one of the largest city squares in the world. It is ringed by amazing structures—Mexico's Metropolitan Cathedral, the National Palace, and the historic wonder of the partially excavated remains of the ancient Aztec capital, Tenochititlán. But Justin was about to alter the landscape with his own monumental starpower.

The night of the concert was awesome—more than 300,000 fans crowded into the Zócalo and the nearby streets where giant TV screens had been set up for viewing Justin's performance. The sound of anticipation was almost deafening. Before the show, Justin tweeted, "The pics of the crowds look CRAZY here in MEXICO CITY!! IM HYPED!! This is going to be fun! MEXICO I LOVE YOU! Te AMO MUCHO!!"

To thank his Mexico City audience, Justin took time before the concert to film a short video on his smartphone camera. "I can't say how thankful I am … This show here in Mexico City, it's going to be incredible. I just wanted to make this video and tell you guys you inspire me just as much as I inspire you. God has really blessed me and he's given me this platform so that I can do as much good as possible and sing my heart out for you guys. I hope to have this journey for a long time."

All the build-up was worth it. Justin rocked the concert and the audience showered him with love, cheers, and tears. Still pumped after the show, Justin once again took to Twitter and shot out, "everything about tonight was special. It is everything we stand for. A lot of emotions but it was worth it. 300,000 people. Te Amo MEXICO. NO ONE CAN EVER TAKE AWAY YOUR DREAMS! BELIEVE. DREAM BIG!"

Gracias!

Once again Justin and his crew gave their all and killed it on stage. You could hear the crowd's appreciation miles away from the Zócalo! Afterwards, Justin released one more thank you—this time on YouTube—"Put on a free show and 300,000 people showed up. A lot of emotions but just wanted to say I wouldn't be here without all of your support. Wanted you to know how I feel. Thanks for everything I hope you chase every dream as you are helping me live mine every day. Thank you."

MuchMusic Video Awards, Toronto, Canada

After his return from Europe and Mexico, Justin took a few days to unwind before picking up speed once again. Then on June 17th, he hit Toronto, Canada for the MuchMusic Video Awards and got a great reception from his fellow Canadians. On the MMVA red carpet, Justin posed for the cameras and stopped to talk to reporters, all the while holding his two-year-old brother, Jaxon.

Justin's first appearance on the MMVA stage that night was to accept the award for "International Video of The Year by a Canadian" for "Boyfriend." "Thank you so much," Justin told the audience. "I want to say thank you so much to my home. I want to say thank you to all my family, my fans. I wouldn't be here without you guys. You guys are amazing. I love you." Later, Justin also won the "UR Fave Artist" award. And then, as the show's main attraction, he closed the festivities with a medley performance of "All Around The World" and "Boyfriend."

Of course, Justin had even more to be proud of that evening—his very own "discovery," Carly Rae Jepsen, was the big winner of the night. She took home three awards for her hit single "Call Me Maybe"— "Video of the Year," "Most Streamed Video of the Year," and "UR Fave—Video."

Introducing his younger brother, Jaxon, to the spotlight, Justin and his School Boy Records artist, Carly Rae Jepsen, stop for the cameras on the MuchMusic Video Awards' red carpet.

Justin shows his dancing swag as he and his backup dancers hit the stage one more time!

At the MMVAs Justin sang "If I was your boyfriend...". There were definitely a lot of girls in the audience wishing he were!

NYC—The Apollo Blows Up!

Justin wanted to continue his free concert series in New York City. Originally his management had planned for him to appear at an outdoor site there, but that didn't work out. So where could they go? How about uptown, to one of Mannhattan's most iconic music venues, the legendary Apollo Theatre in Harlem, a cultural institution in the black community for decades. Some quick maneuvering led the Bieber entourage there on the night of June 18th . . . and thousands of Beliebers followed.

Justin was hyped about taking the same stage that such music greats as Stevie Wonder, the Beatles, and Aretha Franklin had. But he was especially touched that his personal idol, Michael Jackson, had performed there throughout his long career. Before the show, Justin tweeted, "A lot of emotions in the building. This one is special. This one is for MJ."

The night started off in typical Bieber style—energized! The crowd thundered with excitement, dancing, clapping, cheering, and hardly ever sitting down. Ludacris, a surprise special guest, and Justin performed their *Believe* collab, "All Around The World." Then . . . it happened! The power went out! The lights died, the sound faded, the stage instruments and videocameras went dead. And then the fire alarm went off! Security sprang into action to make sure everyone was safe. After they gave the all-clear, Justin's manager, Scooter Braun, told MTV News, "[Justin] walks out, he literally quiets the crowd, and he says, 'I'm sorry the power is out . . . [But] you guys have always had my back. I'm going to sing 'Boyfriend' and you're going to sing it back to me."

Justin ended the show singing with the audience. Awesome! Afterwards, he tweeted, "Me and @ludacris blew up the power at the @ApolloTheater. Haha. Epic. #beastmode . . . A night none of us will ever forget!! That is how u end an #AllAroundTheWorld run!! With no power for the last song . . . my fans sang it 4 me!"

Even though the power went off during Justin's Apollo show, he kept performing along with his dancers, singers, his rap-bud Ludacris—and the audience! "What I saw tonight!" he tweeted after the show. "My fans! My Beliebers! They stepped up for me! I love u! I will never forget znite! That was the way a show should end."

SWAGGY STYLE

The Evolution of Swag

Remember Justin back in 2010? Wide-eyed, baby-faced, and just plain adorable? Cap worn backwards, purple T-shirt, baggy jeans, and kicks — that was his style.

With hits like "Baby," Justin made fans fall in love, and it wasn't long before the Bieber Fever epidemic had swept the globe.

But it's 2012, and in the course of two short years, this baby has come a long way, both with his music and his style. Today, Justin is an iconic force when it comes to fashion, music, and even the English language. While "swag" has long been used by rappers as shorthand for "swagger," Justin uses the term differently, mostly to describe his personal style, and

it's caught on. Now Justin is known as the King of Swag! He's graduated from hip kid next door to trend-setting risk-taker. Today's Justin Bieber swags out to a red carpet affair in designer duds, such as his bright blue MCM x TI$A Perfecto leather jacket, top-label black skinny jeans, and one-of-a-kind high-tops. His everyday attire is a little more low-key, but always distinctively Bieber—designer jeans, leather jacket, gold chain, and dog tags. Justin's preferred color palette is black and white with an occasional splash of bright red, blue or yellow kicks. Needless to say, Justin has definitely developed his own style . . . nobody swags like Bieber when it comes to fashion!

Alterations, Bieber Style

Writer Drew Magary spent several days with Justin for a GQ profile and wrote of one fashion moment he shared with the singer and his friend and former stylist, Ryan Aldred: "We head into his studio, where Aldred greets Bieber and pumps him up for the evening by ripping the sleeves off of his T-shirt while he's still wearing it. OUTTA MY WAY, SLEEVES. This is clearly not the first time they've performed this ritual. It's Bieber's patented entrance move, his talcum powder tossed in the air. Being Justin Bieber means having an endless number of T-shirts to destroy."

Justin shines onstage at his Mexico City concert. Gray-and-silver-studded hoodie, white pants, and gloves are totally Bieber!

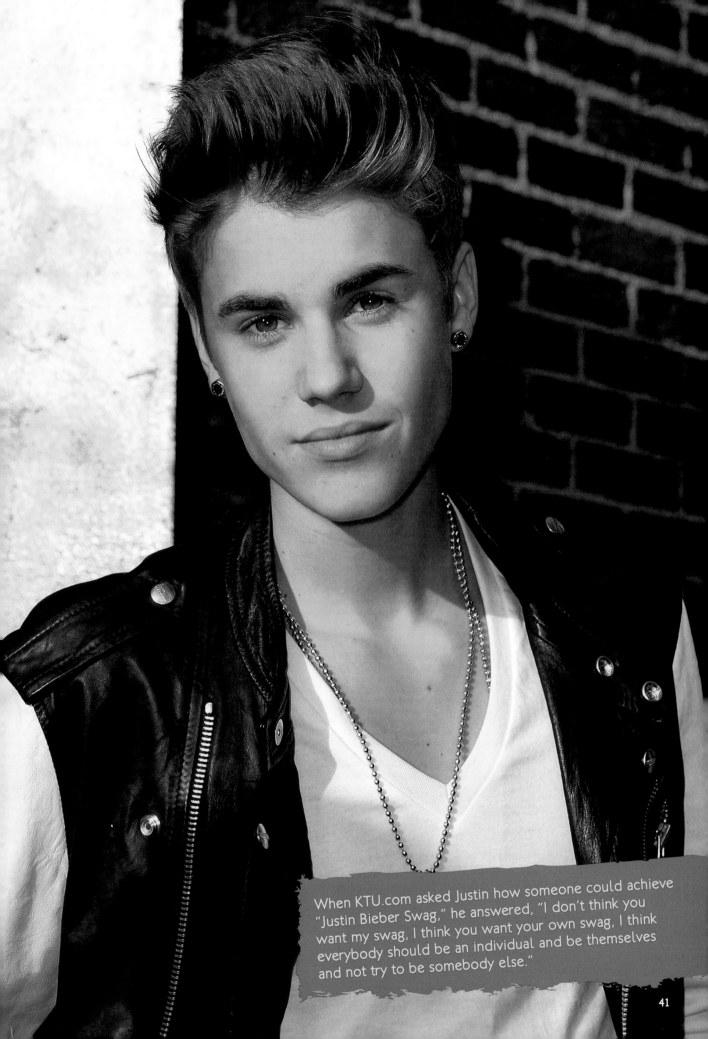

When KTU.com asked Justin how someone could achieve "Justin Bieber Swag," he answered, "I don't think you want my swag, I think you want your own swag, I think everybody should be an individual and be themselves and not try to be somebody else."

Sweet and Swaggy

Justin is one of the very first male celebrities to introduce fragrances for the ladies who love him! That's right . . . he has not one, but two best-selling perfumes, both of which are sold in department stores. The first is Someday, which won the "Elizabeth Taylor Fragrance Celebrity of the Year" award at the 2012 FiFi's—the fragrance industry's equivalent of the Oscar's. His second fragrance, Girlfriend, was released the same week *Believe* hit the stores.

Justin rocks his classic swoop hairstyle along with his version of the animal print trend in June 2012.

Justin talked about his fragrance, Someday, on *The Tonight Show with Jay Leno* in October 2011.

Justin gives his best swag look at the
2012 Billboard Music Awards in Las Vegas.

Look at those lips! Justin appeared on a Spanish TV show.

Staying Swaggy

As his style has matured to match his new adult swagger, Justin has taken charge in the physical fitness arena too. Considering that his dad, Jeremy Bieber, was a former Mixed Martial Arts (MMA) fighter, Justin is no stranger to the gym. Though Justin's own interest in boxing has lasted long enough for one intense training session, Justin works out in other ways as often as he can. His efforts have definitely buffed up his slender frame and he's eager to show it off. He even did a pumped-up photo shoot, which he posted on the video-sharing application Viddy. "Photoshoot this morning . . . now off to day two of rehearsals for billboard. Come get me on viddy," he tweeted to fans.

This attention to fitness is just part of Justin's grand plan to be the best at what he does. Justin believes in giving his all to every fan, every performance, and every project. "I give up a personal life," he told *Complex* magazine in March 2012. "I give up my friends and family to pursue what I love and to make my fans happy. Why would I give up so much to be just another singer? . . . When I release something, I want it to be the best. When I release my fragrance, I want it to be the number-one fragrance. I don't want it to be the ninth-best-selling fragrance. My Christmas album went double-platinum worldwide. Christmas albums don't do that, and that still wasn't good enough for me . . . I feel like it's my responsibility to be the greatest I can be."

Justin at 102.7 KISS FM's Wango Tango concert.

Back to basics for Justin when he sits down for an 18th birthday interview at NYC's Z-100.

Just Justin: Random Faves and Other Stuff

CELL PHONE: iPhone

CAR REMODELING COMPANY: West Coast Customs

CARS: Black Mercedes-Benz Sprinter van, black Smart Car, Silver Fisker Karma, black Batman-themed Cadillac CTS-V coupe, black Range Rover

CANDY: Swedish fish

RESTAURANT: Benihana

VEGETABLE: Broccoli

TATTOOS: An outline of a seagull on his upper left hip, a Jesus Christ image on the back of his left leg, praying hands to the left of and slightly below the Jesus portrait, "Jesus" written in Hebrew on his left chest, "BELIEVE" on his inner left elbow, and a Japanese Kanji symbol which means music, on his inside right forearm.

FIRST LOVE

Justin + Selena = Jelena

Back in February 2011, the rumors of Justin Bieber and Selena Gomez dating were finally confirmed with a photographed kiss at the Oscars' *Vanity Fair* party! Shortly after that, Selena visited the *Late Show with David Letterman,* and revealed the two had first met Hollywood-style. "Actually, his manager called my mom, who's my manager," she told Letterman about their introduction. "I'm blushing!" When the TV host pushed about them dating, Selena said, "He's been in my life for so long, and it's just nice to have someone that understands what you're going through."

After that interview, the couple, nicknamed "JELENA," became more comfortable out in public, and they were often seen walking hand-in-hand, hugging, and yes, even kissing! Of course, because of their busy schedules their dates had to be something special. "Most of our dates have been online," Selena joked with *J-14,* when she admitted that a lot of their time together was, by necessity, via Skype, Twitter, BBMing, and the good old telephone. But when they did have the chance to spend time together, it was the pure definition of romance! Examples? Justin renting the L.A. Staples Center for a private screening of *Titanic* for them . . . Justin hiring a helicopter when they were in Toronto for the MuchMusic Video Awards and going to visit his family in Stratford, Ontario . . . Taking relaxing vacations in Maui, Hawaii, yachting off the coast of St. Lucia, or celebrating their one year

anniversary in Cabo San Lucas, Mexico.

Justin, like Selena, has been very protective of their relationship. When they are out together, he has tried to make sure the paparazzi and crowds haven't gotten too close to her, and he never likes to go into detail about their time together. Neither of them likes to read or even deal with the "Jelena Splits" headlines that are part and parcel of a celebrity romance. The press seems to blow up every little stumble in their relationship and that kind of publicity can put pressure on anyone. However, there are times Justin lets his heart open up—like the time he recalled their very first kiss in an interview with the British magazine *Fabulous.* "My first kiss with Selena was the best of my life," he said. "It was in the car. It was scary and spontaneous and it was just awesome."

And romantic!

Titanic Love Story

When Justin rented out the L.A. Staples Center for a private dinner and screening of *Titanic* just for Selena and himself, it made headlines. "[Selena and I] were fighting a little bit," Justin said in *J-14.* "We ended up being cool and everything was great, but I really wanted to take her somewhere special. . . . She was talking about how she wanted to see *Titanic* again because she hadn't since she was a little girl. Romance isn't dead."

Cute couple! Justin and Selena do basic black at the 2011 American Music Awards. The camera even caught them snuggling as they sat in the first row at the show.

Justin makes sure Selena is with him as they head into the MTV Voices dinner at the 2011 MTV Europe Music Awards.

On the Road and in Love

"What does love feel like? It feels good," Justin told *Fabulous* when asked about LOVE. "If you're really in love, then you should get butterflies. Butterflies and happiness, that's how I feel anyway. But I never like to throw it in my fans' faces. I love my fans and I'd never want to do that to them. It's my private life and I like to keep that separate. I don't have many things that I get to keep to myself but that's one thing. I'm very happy. And I know my fans just want to be happy for me."

Another trip to an airport! This time Justin scooped up Selena as she arrived in Toronto for the MuchMusic Video Awards.

Justin loved it when Selena went with him to visit his family in Ontario. The couple left Justin's grandparents' house after celebrating Justin's dad's 37th birthday.

Justin and Selena enjoyed a quiet-time picnic in L.A.'s Griffith Park.

Selena on Justin

In a cover story for the July 2012 *ELLE*, Selena was asked about her relationship with JB. She wouldn't go into detail about it, and laughingly said, "I'm glad I can say that there are things you don't know about us." But she then added, "If I'll share anything with you, it's that he really is a hopeless romantic."

L.A. Laker fever!

Date Night! Justin and Selena are known to be big basketball fans. At the Staples Center on April 17th to watch the L.A. Lakers play the San Antonio Spurs, they got great seats: courtside. Both had been out of town working—Justin promoting his upcoming album, *Believe,* and Selena filming *Spring Breakers* in Miami—so this date was a bit of a romantic reunion. The 40,000-plus sports fans at the game caught a glimpse when the couple was captured by the mega-screen kiss-cam! Though they only had eyes for each other, they couldn't help but share their good feelings with a little fan who was lucky enough to be sitting right next to her idols—JUSTIN BIEBER and SELENA GOMEZ! Everyone was a winner . . . uh, except for the Lakers, who lost to the Spurs 112 to 91!

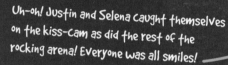
Uh-oh! Justin and Selena caught themselves on the kiss-cam as did the rest of the rocking arena! Everyone was all smiles!

Selena isn't the only one getting attention! Definitely a night to remember for this little girl.

Well, they might as well give the people a little PDA! You could practically hear a 100-decibel "Awwwww!!!!" from the sports fans!

THE WORLD'S BEST BOYFRIEND

What's the definition of a "good boyfriend"? Just ask millions of girls worldwide—it's JUSTIN BIEBER, of course! But there are two sides of boyfriend Justin right now. First there is the hit, "Boyfriend," which was the first single from his album *Believe*. And then there is Justin, the real-life BF. Let's take a peek at both.

Behind the Scenes Boyfriend Facts

★ MUSTANG MAYHEM: "We started off with the car stunts. We wrecked that car by the way; both of those Mustangs were pretty shot after this video, completely shot after this video." (Director X to MTV News)

★ GOLD SHOES: "I did pick out those swaggy gold shoes. They spray-painted them gold. That's what I'm going to do: I'm gonna start wearing gold shoes all the time." (Justin to MTV News)

★ YOUTUBE RECORD: By May 3rd "Boyfriend" had 8 million views on YouTube alone, which broke the record for single-day statistics, and within a week it had more than 17 million hits. (*Billboard*)

★ JAMES "JUSTIN" DEAN: "Justin's new look, he's kind of got a James Dean thing going here. That's really Justin driving that Mustang . . . and he did all the stunts by himself, completely." (Director X to MTV News)

★ GIRLFRIEND: Actress Rachel Barnes only *played* Justin's GF—"I, myself, am already married. I'm a Belieber, but he's not my boyfriend. It's been great to be part of the Bieber madness . . . even if only for a song." (MTV News)

"The song definitely comes from my heart. I'll never let you go if you're my girlfriend, I promise," Justin told E! online about "Boyfriend."

A real car lover, Justin was hyped about driving the classic Mustangs!

"Boyfriend"

As the first single, "Boyfriend" set the perfect tone for the rest of the album. It showed Justin's growing musical maturity and was also the kind of song everyone could blast and sing along to. Justin was so involved in the production of this single that he got "additional writing" credits. "I want people to know that I'm really about the music, and not just putting out songs," Justin explained to *Billboard*. "This was the perfect first single where I pushed myself, but it wasn't too 'out there' and it had a catchy hook."

Justin and his crew worked the release like pure magic. On March 1st he teased his fans with a snippet on *The Ellen DeGeneres Show*. Then, on March 16th, Justin released two photos of himself and asked his fans to tweet-vote the one they wanted to be the cover art for "Believe." One shot had Justin looking straight into the camera with his right hand running through his hair. The other was Justin looking down with his hands at his side. The Twitter-world blew up and on March 19th the "hand–in–hair" shot won! "Boyfriend" was released on March 26th—and it was an instant hit!

On May 8th, Justin tweeted, "BIG DAY TODAY. Performing #BOYFRIEND for the first time Live on the FINALE of @NBCTheVoice." That night, JB was finally able to show everyone just how hot "Boyfriend" really was.

Many people think Rachel Barnes, his love interest in the "Boyfriend" video, bears a striking resemblance to Selena Gomez

The Video

Fans had to wait till May 8th to see a live performance of "Boyfriend," but on May 3rd the music video hit the airwaves. Justin premiered it on *MTV First: Justin Bieber* and afterwards he sat down with MTV's Sway to discuss "Boyfriend" and *Believe*. The buzz was deafening!

In the "Boyfriend" video, Justin drives a muscle car, snuggles next to a dead ringer for Selena Gomez, gets his dance on at an L.A. rooftop party. "Boyfriend" director, Director X, told MTV News' Sway, "It was just cars and the simplicity that they liked. Cars, girls, just young people hanging out, having fun, that kind of thing. When I heard it, I thought that's what it should be."

"He's a good kid. He comes to work, gets the job done, dedicated to the gig. I mean, I like him." (Director X to MTV News)

Director X said that Justin did all of his driving in "Boyfriend." Here, Justin and the crew prepare for a shot.

"We're seeing [Justin] grow," Director X told MTV News. "It's not the same old Justin."

Real Life Boyfriend

"I think it's important to make all women feel like they're princesses, because every girl is a princess. I'm serious," Justin told *Seventeen*.

Obviously Justin has given a lot of thought to being a good boyfriend and he summed it up in five easy tips when he talked to MTV News on the "Boyfriend" set. "I don't know if I'm even the best boyfriend, but I can give a few suggestions. I think being honest and patient, because girls can be tough sometimes, so you just got to be patient. That's two. Forgive, and have fun, because it's about having fun. . . . Last one? Be faithful."

Sounds like good advice!

Justin's James Dean-inspired look.

"I'm still learning about different things. Girls, my music. I'm not all the way there. I'm at a stage, I'm growing. My fans are growing with me. I want to make music that reflects that." (the *Today* show)

Justin and Rachel get cozy filming a scene for the "Boyfriend" video.

Justin on the set of the "Boyfriend" video.

GIRLS ON JUSTIN'S SPEED DIAL

Justin can't deny that he is an object of affection for girls all around the world. And neither can Selena! But that's something they both deal with . . . and sometimes laugh about together. Of course every time Justin is photographed or videotaped with another girl, especially a celebrity, you can count on cyber-city and tabloid-town to broadcast it in a matter of minutes. Unfortunately for Justin, living in the public eye just comes with the territory. He understands what it means to be a SUPERSTAR, and he takes it all in stride. With a girlfriend who knows where he stands, a family who understands and supports him, and friends who keep him grounded, Justin seems to have the best of both worlds.

Krazy for Katy Perry

A big fan of Justin's, singer Katy Perry has always supported him as a singer and as a celebrity. While promoting her autobiographical film, *Part of Me 3D*, in June, Justin's name came up during an interview on the Dallas-area radio show *Kidd Kraddick In The Morning* (FF 2:10). "I love Justin Bieber," she said. "He can do no wrong in my eyes."

About Katy, well, Justin will never forget when Katy kissed him on the cheek at the 2010 American Music Awards. He told *Access Hollywood*, "She's funny. She's hot, she's good, she's hot. She's hot, she's gorgeous. It's funny. She's cool." About the kiss, he said, "It just happened. She kissed me on the cheek and I was like 'yeah, let's get it.'"

Katy & Justin

Tons of Fun with Taylor Swift

Well-known pals Justin and Taylor have been able to enjoy both personal and professional moments together. They collaborated on a song that didn't make it onto *Believe*, but according to Selena, "it was beautiful." What wasn't so beautiful was Taylor's reaction when Justin debuted the revamped MTV series, *Punk'd*. After Justin fooled her into thinking a fireworks display she set off caught a wedding party boat on fire, Taylor freaked . . . until the *Punk'd* gang revealed the joke. After she got it, she started to laugh, and Justin told Chicago's *J & Julian Morning Show* at B96, "She was super sweet. You could tell how genuine she was about caring about the situation. She was fun to get."

Taylor even tweeted Justin after she was punked, congratulating him. "@justinbieber got me good. It was masterful. And sort of traumatic. " also saying "Well played, @justinbieber. I was truly terrified."

Taylor & Justin

Kim & Justin

Kicking it with Kim Kardashian

Justin and reality TV star Kim Kardashian first met when they did a photo shoot for *Elle* magazine back in 2010. As some of the photos began to surface online, rumors that the two were dating began to circulate as well. When the magazine was just about to hit the stands, Kim wrote on her official blog, "Remember those paparazzi pics of me and Justin Bieber in the Bahamas!? Well, I can now reveal that we were shooting for *Elle* Magazine! I just received the pics from the shoot and I absolutely LOVE how they turned out! . . . Justin and I had such a fun time together at the shoot."

After *Elle* hit the stands, Kim was interviewed on *Lopez Tonight* and told host George Lopez, "[Justin] definitely has this swag to him. You just have to meet him. I thought that the shoot was all in fun. We had a good time."

Chillin With Ellen DeGeneres

Over the years, Justin and the host of *The Ellen DeGeneres Show* have become very good friends. He has celebrated some of the biggest moments of his life on Ellen's show, including his 18th birthday, his high school graduation, introducing the world to his new protégé Carly Rae Jepsen, and much, much more. It was there that he first talked about his "friendship" with Selena Gomez. Ellen's show is Justin's place to go when he wants to send info out to his fans—so it wasn't a surprise that on May 23, 2012, he made an exciting statement. "I'm announcing my tour!" Justin told the audience. "We have the dates." Then, Ellen revealed that everyone had two tickets under their seats for his Believe tour!

Of course, Ellen had more on her mind than just the tour—the show was taped shortly after Justin and Selena were photographed kissing at the L.A. Lakers game. "[Did] you ever really get a chance to watch the game?" Ellen asked. Justin just laughed!

Ellen DeGeneres

Ha-ha with Hayden Panettiere

When Justin graced the cover of *Vanity Fair*'s February 2011 issue, actress Hayden Panettiere added her congratulations via a video for *Vanity Fair*'s Daily Blog. First she primped her short blond hair and laughed, "My hair is Bieber'd!" Then, holding the magazine, she looked right into the camera and said, "What a lucky dude! Congratulations! Sixteen years old . . . same age as my little brother!"

Hayden & Justin

Avalanna & Justin

Meet Avalanna Routh . . . Mrs. Bieber!

Little six-year-old Avalanna Routh of Boston, Massachusetts, first met her idol, Justin Bieber, on Valentine's Day 2012. Avalanna was undergoing chemotherapy and radiation for an aggressive form of brain cancer and her family had posted a Facebook request to Justin for her to meet him. When Justin heard about it, he immediately made arrangements to have Avalanna and her family flown to New York City to meet him on Valentine's Day.

And it wasn't just a quick meet-and-greet! Justin spent the whole afternoon with Avalanna. They played board games, ate Valentine's snacks . . . it was even agreed that Avalanna would be called "Mrs. Bieber" from then on!

After their "date," Justin tweeted "That was one of the best things i have ever done. she was AWESOME! Feeling really inspired now! . . . #MrsBieber really inspired me.'

All of Justin's fans fell in love with Avalanna and pretty soon she was trending on Twitter! Avalanna and Justin keep in touch on a specially set-up Facebook page and on iChat. When the singer told her he was going to perform on the *Today* show to promote *Believe*, he asked if she wanted to come. Of course she did! So once again, the Routh family headed to The Big Apple ... first stop, the *Today* show! Needless to say it was a happy reunion for Mr. and Mrs. Bieber. BTW, it's official: "There was a paper cutout of me and she did the whole wedding with the paper cutout," Justin told the *Today* show's Matt Lauer during his interview!

Carly Rae Jepsen
He Will Call Her . . . No Maybes About It!

It's always cool to have a successful mentor supporting you, but it's especially helpful in the music biz. No one knows this better than Justin Bieber—after all, his mentor was Usher. You can't get any better than that. Well, maybe you can match that if you are Canadian singer Carly Rae Jepsen and Justin Bieber is your mentor! It was only a matter of months between the time Justin first heard Carly Rae's "Call Me Maybe" on his car radio during his Canadian Christmas vacay and when he helped her achieve international success. "I immediately fell in love with the song," Justin told *J-14*. So it wasn't surprising that he tweeted his GF, Selena, about it and word spread like wildfire. Carly Rae's sister, Katie, called her and told her that Justin Bieber and Selena Gomez were tweeting about "Call Me Maybe," and at that point, Carly Rae told *J-14*, "My whole life changed."

Carly Rae enjoyed the YouTube viral success of the "cover" video of "Call Me Maybe," which featured Justin, Selena, Ashley Tisdale, Alfredo Flores, Big Time Rush's Kendall Schmidt, Carlos Pena, Logan Henderson, and more, dancing around, going crazy, and lip-synching to the song! Meanwhile, Justin was taking care of business, too, and signed Carly Rae to School Boy Records. "Call Me Maybe" soon reached the *Billboard* Hot 100 Singles Number One spot in the U.S., Canada, and other countries around the world.

Two days after the cover of "Call Me Maybe" was posted, Carly Rae was in L.A. to meet Justin. "I was so nervous, but he was very down-to-earth," Carly Rae told *J-14*. "He played me one song and it was the loveliest song I'd ever heard, so I ended up going into the studio with him. That was literally our introduction."

It didn't stop there. Carly Rae hit the stage with Justin in June when he was performing for a crowd of 80,000 at the Capital FM Summertime Ball part of his mini-promo tour. Justin danced around as Carly Rae wowed the audience with "Call Me Maybe." Later that month, Justin and Carly Rae shared the honors on stage once again at the MuchMusic Video Awards, where Carly Rae won the "Video of the Year" and "UR Fave Video of the Year" awards for "Call Me Maybe." It was even announced that Carly Rae would be opening for Justin when his *Believe* tour kicks off. Not bad for a newcomer!

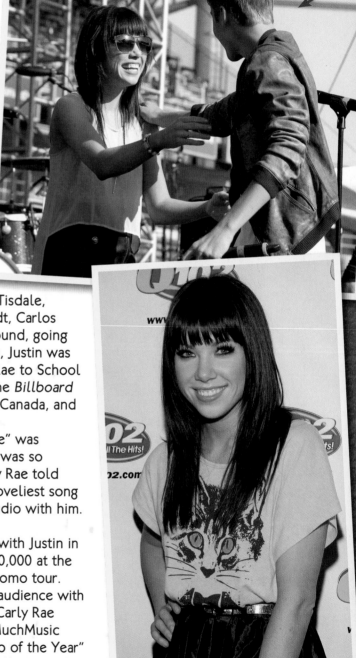

"I feel so lucky," Carly Rae told *J-14* of her whirlwind success. "It's like a movie that I'm just randomly in."

"[Carly Rae's] a great singer, she's funny and charismatic," Justin said on Chicago's J & Julian Morning Show at B96. "She's a cool girl. I think other girls can relate to her. She's got a great song."

JB . . . MUSIC MAN

Believe Makes a Bang

It didn't take more than one week for Bieber and his new album to make music history. *Believe* was Justin's fourth album to debut at number one on the *Billboard 200* chart—*My World 2.0*, *Never Say Never: The Remixes*, and *Under The Mistletoe* were the others—and in its first week out, it sold more than 374,000 copies.

According to Yahoo Music, "Bieber is the first artist in chart history to land four #1 albums or EPs while still in his teens." MTV News reported, "Experts are predicting that not only will JB top the tally, but he's headed for his best first week ever and the likely crown of the year's biggest debut."

Justin knew that *Believe* had the potential to be a real game-changer, but it was his hard work and willingness to collaborate that made the album so successful. "You know, I think a lot of times with big superstars, they don't always deliver on that big album," manager Scooter Braun told MTV News. "They don't meet the expectation . . . sometimes it's because they're superstars. Maybe they think they know it all and they don't want to listen to anyone else's input, and sometimes that works and sometimes that doesn't. Justin was really humble about this. He probably wrote 200 songs and we just kept working and working and narrowing it down. And there were so many [songs] that didn't even make it that we'll save for something else. I think when it was all said and done, there wasn't one person who listened to that album all the whole way through and thought that we didn't have something special and really great and something that didn't just reach the teenagers, but everyone— without losing the teenagers."

The Dream Team: manager Scooter Braun, vocal coach Jan Smith, Justin, and mentor Usher. Here they are at the 33rd Annual Georgia Music Hall of Fame Awards in 2011.

Believe (Deluxe Edition) Track List

"All Around The World" (featuring Ludacris)

"Boyfriend"

"As Long As You Love Me" (featuring Big Sean)

"Catching Feelings"

"Take You"

"Right Here" (featuring Drake)

"Fall"

"Die In Your Arms"

"Thought Of You"

"Beauty And A Beat" (featuring Nicki Minaj)

"One Love"

"Be Alright"

"Believe"

"Out Of Town Girl"

"She Don't Like The Lights"

"Maria"

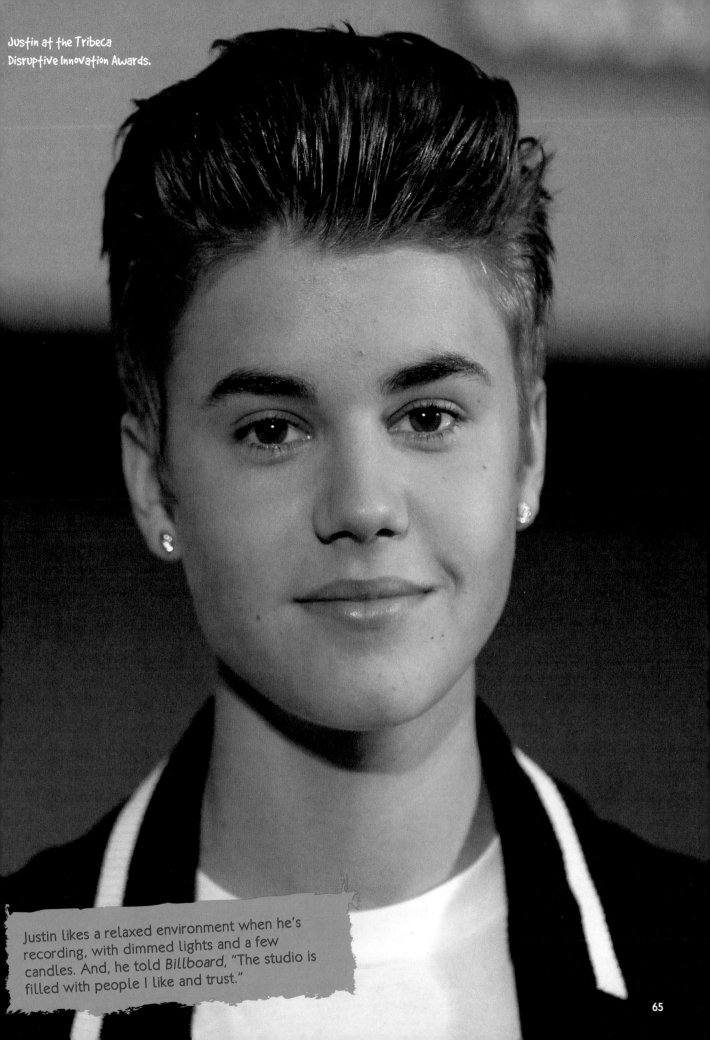

Justin at the Tribeca Disruptive Innovation Awards.

Justin likes a relaxed environment when he's recording, with dimmed lights and a few candles. And, he told *Billboard*, "The studio is filled with people I like and trust."

The Master Musician's Amazing Week

"I feel great. I'm really happy," Justin told *Access Hollywood* just days after *Believe* was released. "The album turned out great and the fans love it and the critics love it and everyone's been raving about it. So, it's been an amazing week so far."

Indeed, "amazing" may only begin to describe Justin's life around the time of his album release. The Friday before *Believe* hit stores, JB was interviewed by Matt Lauer on the *Today* show and performed with Big Sean for thousands of Beliebers at the morning show's Rockefeller Plaza. Then, the week of the release, Justin appeared on the *Late Show with David Letterman*, had a two-night NBC special documentary, *Justin Bieber: All Around The World*, and paired with TV host and friend Jimmy Fallon on YouTube for a question-and-answer session. Of course, there were the dozens of TV and radio interviews for Justin, so it was natural that someone should ask, "Are you tired?" In an interview with *Access Hollywood*, Justin laughed and answered, "No, I don't get tired. I'm actually a robot, so . . . No, of course, I get tired, yeah. I get tired. . . . [But] I'm pretty laid back. I try to just take everything day by day and everything happens for a reason."

If Bieber was a machine for those months of tireless work on the album, we know that he felt a sense of accomplishment and pride when the 16-track album finally dropped and received praise from critics and fans alike. Hours of studio time with Drake, Nicki Minaj, Ludacris, Big Sean, will.i.am, and more, finally paid off. When news started leaking about these collabs before the album's release, fans and music critics wondered what direction the album would take. Justin only revealed that it was going to be "more mature."

He forgot to mention "swaggy," too.

Justin heads into the studio on April 2012 to put some finishing touches on Believe.

The Making of Believe

"[Justin] and I are both very competitive, and he'd always look at me and go, 'This is the make-it-or-break-it album, and you got to push me. You got to tell me if I'm not good enough, and I might argue' . . . so I really, really pushed him, and we took this album really seriously. But I also had to give room to grow. Sometimes I'd put him in writing sessions for two weeks, and we'd get one song out of it, and it was just because he had to find that place for himself and that music. As the process went on, he really started hitting his stride. . . . And I think everyone has a different favorite, but the one common thread is you don't dislike any songs."
—Scooter Braun (MTV News)

Justin Bieber's Believe Debuts at No. 1 in 30 Countries!

Justin Believes! At the 2012 Billboard Awards, Justin lets his fans know he's their "Boyfriend."

Long-time friends, Canadian boys Justin and Drake hit the stage together at the 22nd Annual MuchMusic Video Awards in 2011.

Believe's Collabs

When the *My World* EP first came out, Justin was a pop singer, but with the releases of *My World 2.0* and *Never Say Never: The Remixes*, the wonder boy from Canada has grown and evolved. Not only have his fans enjoyed watching Justin flex his budding hip-hop muscles, but the heavyweights of the hip-hop world have noticed them too. Sean Kingston, Kanye West, Drake, Ludacris, Lil Wayne, Raekwon, Nicki Minaj, and many others have welcomed him into their fold. Justin's first self-tited rapper persona, Shawty Mane, didn't last long—it was 2 Chainz who solidified JB's hip-hop cred and dubbed him "Lil Swaggy."

Justin and Nicki Minaj at the 2011 BET Awards in 2011.

Justin and Big Sean rocked Rockefeller Plaza live on the *Today* show in June 2012.

Major Stops on Justin's Hip-Hop Road

"Baby" featuring Ludacris—Luda dropped his raps on the track

"Runaway Love" Remix featuring Kanye West and Raekwon—Justin hooks up with two of hip-hop's mega stars

"Speaking In Tongues"—Justin, as Shawty Mane, rapped freestyle over Vado and Cam'ron's single

"Ladies Love Me"—Justin raps again as Shawty Mane on this Chris Brown single from Boy In Detention.

"Boyfriend" Remix with the Ying Yang Twins—the Twins spit a rap before Justin's rap starts the song.

"Boyfriend" Remix featuring 2 Chainz—the ATL master rapped a verse on Justin's single, and named him "Lil Swaggy."

Justin with Ludacris at the 2011 Luda Day Weekend, which included music, fun, and a little basketball!

FUN STUFF WITH JUSTIN

With all those outsized personas—Justin Bieber, JB, JayBee, Biebs, Shawty Mane, Lil Swaggy, and more—it's hard to believe that Justin is only 18 years old. He's still a teenager, and even his non-stop megastar lifestyle seems to have trouble keeping up with him. If you've seen the NBC documentary *Justin Bieber: All Around The World,* you may understand what Justin's schedule is like. He's always on the go, but those around him try to make sure he has some time to just relax and enjoy himself. The documentary shows Justin shooting some hoops, hanging out with friends, and, yes, even sleeping! But when he's not on tour, Justin spends his time just like any other 18-year-old would: eating at restaurants, going to movies, playing sports, visiting his family and friends, and, unlike most other kids his age, spending time with his fans.

On the following pages, you will see Justin just being Justin . . . and, finally, enjoying some free time!

When Justin and guitarist Dan Kanter pulled up in a van to *The Tonight Show* studio parking lot, they were greeted by fans waiting to catch an in-the-flesh glimpse of JB. They had no time to spare before he taped his appearance, but afterwards Justin gave his Beliebers an impromptu mini-concert. The cell phones were flashing and the crowd sang along.

When Justin showed off his new ink—BELIEVE on his inner arm—on the *Late Show with David Letterman*, he got some grief from the TV host. Letterman advised Justin not to get too many tattoos: "Do me a favor—don't go nuts, you know what I mean?" But Justin stuck up for himself. He explained that he got his "Believe" tattoo so that he would always remember the release and success of his album!

During Justin's *All Around The World* mini-tour, he made a stop in Spain. One of his visits was to the very popular TV variety show *El Hormiguero*. In his segment, Bieber hopped on a Segway scooter and zipped around the set. Wonder if Justin got one for his new house. . .

During a 2011 visit to his hometown in Canada, Justin joined his old soccer team, Stratford City Soccer, for a game. Justin played for a short time at the start of the second half, but he must have been a little out of shape, because five minutes into it, he limped off the field and sat on the sideline with Selena and his family. He still had fun!

Justin knew he was a target for Nickelodeon's famous green slime at the 2012 Kids' Choice Awards, but a guy can hope, right? JB had already made it through most of the show unscathed when he went up to accept the award for "Favorite Male Singer." There, on stage, he got slimed at full blast! So did Will Smith, who held him under the spray. The audience probably enjoyed it more than Justin and Will did.

Just chillin'! Of skateboarding at Lil Wayne's Miami house, Justin told MTV News, "I went down to Miami and to his house. We just skated, and I got mad respect from Wayne. He has this rail at his house, and he's had pros come to the house and no one has tried it because it's pretty sketchy. So I decided that I was going to try it. So I went down, hit the rail, and I landed it. He went crazy saying, 'Ohhh, I didn't know you were like that!'"

When Justin was filming his 2011 *Justin Bieber: Home For the Holidays* Christmas special, he stopped by the Air Canada Centre to check out the NHL's Toronto Maple Leafs. Once again, Justin got to relive some of his favorite childhood memories—he got out on the ice and played with some of the Maple Leafs players. Looks like fun!

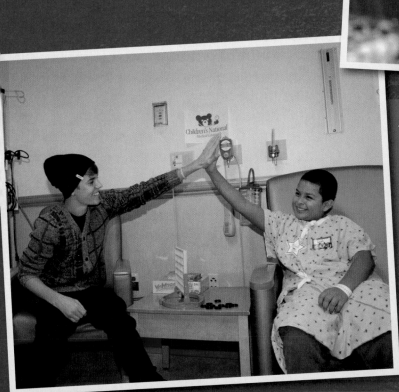

Justin high-fives a patient at the Children's National Medical Center in Washington, D.C. in 2011. In town for Bieber's *Christmas in Washington* concert, Justin and GF Selena made a surprise visit to the hospital to lift the kids' spirits over the holidays. "The kids loved them!" Jacqueline Bowens, the V.P. of External Affairs at the hospital, told *Hollywood Life*. "It was a surprise for them. Justin spent quality time with all of the kids, talked to them, took pictures with them, and sang to them." That's the definition of fun!

JUSTIN'S ROOTS

O, Canada!

Justin is very proud of his Canadian roots, but with his 24/7 always-on-the-go schedule, he doesn't get to spend as much time in the Maple Leaf country as he would like. Because his parents split when he was only ten months old, growing up wasn't easy for Justin. His dad worked in construction back then and often took out-of-town jobs. His mom, Pattie, worked hard not only to financially support them, but to make Justin feel happy and secure in their Stratford, Ontario home. "We lived in public housing, and there were no luxuries at our little apartment, but it never occurred to me that we were poor," Justin wrote in his autobiography, *Justin Bieber: First Step 2 Forever.* "We had each other, which was everything we needed."

Justin's maternal grandparents, Bruce and Diane Dale, were also a big part of his young life. Some of Justin's best memories include going fishing with his grandfather, spending time at his great-grandfather's cabin on Star Lake in Ontario, Christmas dinner with his family at his grandparents' house, playing hockey and soccer with his friends, and just being a typical Canadian kid.

Bieber's life today is very different, to say the least. In his book, Justin wrote, ". . . when I was little, I longed for a 'normal' life with a 'normal' family, and there's no way that's ever going to happen now. There's a circus going on around me everywhere I go, which makes it hard on my family sometimes. . . . You won't hear me complain about how my life is going, but I hope someday I'll be out on Star Lake with my own grandkid, reeling in brown trout and telling stories about how all of us would get together by the fire pit in the evening, everybody laughing and talking at once."

These days, Justin is traveling the world, meeting fans and famous celebrities, and making new memories, but he knows none of it would be possible without the strong roots he grew back in Stratford, Ontario.

Read on to meet the people who were there for him from the beginning.

(Left to right): Justin's half sister, Jazmyn Bieber; his dad, Jeremy Bieber; Justin; his mom, Pattie Mallette. Though Justin's parents divorced when he was young, they always shared a love for their son. Here, they share the excitement of the premiere of his movie, Never Say Never.

Awww! Justin gives his half-brother, Jaxon, a big kiss on the red carpet of the 2012 MuchMusic Video Awards. Big bro is getting little bro used to the fans!

A Closer Look

Justin's NBC documentary, *Justin Bieber: All Around The World*, gives a behind-the-scenes look into the life of the performer—the rehearsals, the fans, the performances and much more. There are some private moments too, like when his dad, little brother, Jaxon, and little sister, Jazmyn, join him for the Spain leg of the tour. After a show, Justin returns to his dressing room to see Jazmyn fast asleep on the couch. "Just being able to come back at the end of the night and see my little sister, it's amazing," he says. He crawls onto the couch and cuddles little Jazmyn. You can feel the love!

In the same documentary, you also see Justin return home to Stratford, where he visits his old haunts, including the steps of the Avon Theatre. Once again, Justin becomes the "busker" of old, and performs for a surprised crowd of fans. Justin is flooded with fond memories and love from his hometown. The experience is emotional and Justin announces, "For me, it's important I never forget where I came from."

Back home in Canada, Justin performed a 2011 Christmas concert in Toronto. The guest of honor? His half-sister, Jazmyn!

Justin's Hometown Faves

SPORTS TEAM: NHL's Maple Leafs

CANDY: Caramilk bars

RESTAURANT: Swiss Chalet—he loves the quarter chicken dinner

MUSICAL LANDMARK: The Avon Theatre, where Justin performed for donations— on the steps—when he was a tween

BIRD: The Swan, Stratford's honorary avian ambassador

SINGING COMPETITION: The Stratford Star competition, where Justin came in second when he was 12 years old

BEST FRIENDS: Ryan Butler and Chaz Somers

If you think Justin leads a glamorous life you're right! He and mom, Pattie, were all smiles posing for the photogs with Vogue Editor-in-Chief Anna Wintour at the 2011 Fashion's Night Out party at the Dolce & Gabbana boutique.

Does Justin have a twin? Of course not! Pattie stands between her son (left) and a life-size wax sculpture at Madame Tussauds in London.

"I miss home ... but it's all worth it. I get to do so many other things that I wouldn't get to experience. It's been really a blessing. I have definitely changed over the last few years, and I think it's for the good. I think that I'm getting more mature. But as far as me as a person, I think I'll always be the same person."—Justin (Justin Bieber: All Around The World)

Justin has everything he needs when he arrives in Taiwan: his mom, Pattie, his headphones, and his skateboard!

Pattie Mallette: Mom of the Year

Pattie was only 18 when she had Justin—that's right, the same age Justin is now—so she understands what it means to grow up fast. Although their personal experiences have been very different, Justin and his mom have both learned to sacrifice childhood fun for adult responsibility. It may have taken some growing pains, but Justin understands that this is one of the reasons they are so close. "I admire my mom so much for how she stepped up to meet all the challenges in her life," Justin wrote in *Justin Bieber: First Step 2 Forever*.

Not only did Pattie give Justin a loving home, but she also created an atmosphere that encouraged his musical talents. She always had her favorite music playing—especially Boyz II Men. By the time Justin was five, he was developing his piano skills and could already hold his own behind a drum set. Pattie and one of her musician friends, Nathan McKay—Justin's grandparents dubbed him "the Lion King" because he had a bushy beard—put on a small benefit in a local bar to raise money for Justin's first drum kit. The result? JB's first real set of drums, which included a trap set and kick drum, floor toms, snare, hi-hat and boom cymbal.

Of those days, Justin wrote, "My mom is an absolute sweetheart who has this vivacious, goofy personality, so there were always a lot of interesting, artsy people hanging around our place. I think artsy people who can't afford to go anywhere tend to hang out in the living room of the coolest person, playing guitars and talking about philosophy and whatever, and that's the living room I grew up in."

Even today, Justin still thinks Pattie is the coolest person around!

Pattie travels almost as much as her son! Here she's leaving LAX enroute to meet Justin.

Happy Mother's Day

Justin's song, "Turn To You," was a Mother's Day 2012 tribute to his mom. Some of the lyrics go, "You were just my age when you had me, Mom. You were so brave."

Pattie was proud that her son wrote a special song for her, but she was even more proud when she learned what he planned to do with it. "The proceeds will go to help other single moms," he tweeted. ". . . help moms in need. Give them strength. Thank u mom."

One of the charities receiving money from "Turn To You," is Ontario's Bethesda Centre. Pattie told E! Online, "If it weren't for Bethesda, I'm not sure where Justin or I would be. Bethesda gave us a chance."

JUSTIN IN THE SPOTLIGHT

He Answers His Fans Most-Asked Questions

Everywhere Justin goes, reporters, photographers, and fans shout out questions about his music, his family, his romantic life, and everything else you can think of. When he can, Justin will stop and answer on the fly, but he's more comfortable taking questions in a formal interview session. Even in a more official setting though, Justin will interject his own questions, and definitely a few of his own jokes. That's Justin just being Justin.

Check out some new and old thoughts and musings to various sources from the golden boy!

On his favorite songs...

A: His own song, "Never Say Never": "In a way, it inspired the movie, which is basically about me, a small-town kid, being able to live his dreams and be successful. The message is, 'Don't ever give up,' so I think it was perfect for that."

"Man In The Mirror" by Michael Jackson: "You can feel the emotion in what he's saying and how it's about looking into yourself. The message behind it is great. It's a really inspiring song."

"I Believe I Can Fly" by R. Kelly: "This song is kind of like 'Never Say Never,' where anything is possible and you just have to believe. It's definitely uplifting."

"Dear God" by Boyz II Men: "My mom has been listening to Boyz II Men ever since I was little. It was always on in the house. Now this song is in my iTunes."

His song, "Down To Earth": "It's about my parents splitting up when I was really little and about the struggles I went through and am still going through. I think that's inspiring because so many kids' parents are divorced nowadays." (All from *Bop*)

Justin stops for photos and questions during his *Today* show appearance.

On whether he wishes he were just a normal kid back in Canada. . .

A: "You know, the grass is always greener. If I [were] in Canada, I'd be wishing I was here doing all this stuff. I'm really happy to be where I am and I wouldn't trade it for the world." (*Sunday* Magazine)

On specific phobias. . .

A: "I hate getting sticky stuff on my hands. I've always had, like, a phobia—not a phobia, but if I get stuff on my hands, I have to have a washcloth to wash my hands because it's so annoying." (*The Sunday Times*)

On being famous and having a relationship with a girl. . .

A: "It is not easy to be so young and to have a relationship with someone that doesn't stay private. But, well, I am a public personality, it is what I wanted, so I have to deal with it." (MTV News)

On his music now. . .

A: "With my music it doesn't stay in a box. Everything is so different and that's why I'm so happy with [Believe]. Everything doesn't sound the same, everything's different and [after] each song you won't expect the next song to happen." (digitalspy.com)

Wonder who Justin is talking to? Maybe it's Scooter asking him where he is!

On missing the prom...

A: Fan Caty Elder invited him to her prom, but he couldn't make it. "So, I said, 'I need you to fly to the *Billboard Awards* and you can be my date.' . . . I thought it would be fun."(people.com)

On whether he's worried about One Direction stealing his fans...

A: "I don't think anyone is taking my fans. I'm all for sharing. I think music is a great thing and a universal language. I have the greatest fans in the world. They are never going to betray me. They can like whoever they want." (company.co.uk)

On whether he prefers performing on stage or working in the studio...

A: Every fan is so special to me. I love being in the studio, but not as much as I love performing live because that's when I get to connect with [my fans]." (Justin Bieber: *First Step 2 Forever*)

On comparing Scooter Braun to a chess player...

A: "He treats life like chess, always eight moves ahead." (*The Big Book of Bieber*)

On his good friend and Canadian pal, Ryan Butler... and whether fame changed their relationship...

A: "[Fame] hasn't really changed my life. We are still as good friends as we were before." (Justin's official website)

On performing at the 2012 Billboard Music Awards along with Carly Rae Jepsen and Usher...

A: "This performance is going to be fun. I practiced a lot in the dance studio. I've been working hard, and I can't wait to show the fans... [It's] not a competition. It's all love. We're all a family. Carly is my artist, and I'm Usher's artist, so it's kind of cool that we're all performing here, together." (MTV News)

When back home in Canada making Justin Bieber: Home For The Holidays, Justin stopped by the Daily Bread Food Bank. Fans couldn't stay away!

On whether he's ever been heartbroken...

A: "I haven't gone through it, so I don't really know what it's about. I don't think anyone wants to have heartbreak. I haven't been in that deep place yet, but I'm still looking. I'm still learning every day." (*Seventeen*)

On Justin's relationship with Usher...

A: "What's great is that in Usher, I have a mentor that's been doing it so long and has been successful in everything that he's done. He's made some mistakes, too, but he's learned from them, so he can tell me what to do and what not to do." (*Billboard* Music Awards Special)

On how he plans to stay on top...

A: "Once you're on top, people wonder when you'll fall. I have to keep working hard." (digitalspy.com)

On whether he ever feels pressured into making a decision...

A: "Here's the thing—I'm my own person. I don't make my decisions based around what people are going to think about me. I make them based on what I want to do and who I think I want to be. If none of this was happening, if there were no cameras around me, that's the kind of person I'd want to be—a good person." (*Sunday* Magazine)

Justin sits down for an interview with NYC Z100 DJ, Elvis Duran.

While appearing on the Spainish TV show, El Hormiguero, Justin stood at the window to salute his fans!

JUSTIN'S SHOW BIZ BUDS

Justin is proud of the fact that he has remained good friends with the people who've known him his whole life, despite how famous he has become. But while Justin hasn't forgotten those who have been there for him since the very beginning, it's no surprise that he's made a lot of new friends too. . . show biz friends. After all, the people Justin meets most often nowadays are celebrities like him.

Anyone who reads Justin headlines knows that he likes to pull pranks on other celebs with buds like Jaden Smith, TV host Jimmy Fallon, and Ashton Kutcher, that he looks up to Usher as a mentor, and that he enjoys spending time with pals like Ryan Seacrest and Sean Kingston. Indeed, Justin's list of friends reads like a Who's Who in Hollywood—but don't doubt him for a second. If you are a friend of Justin's, you are a friend for life!

Diggy Simmons & Justin

Justin made sure to talk to his friend and up-and-coming artist, Diggy Simmons, at the 2011 BET Awards. Perhaps he was offering Diggy some advice about being a teen heartthrob.

Will Ferrell & Justin

A big Will Ferrell fan, Justin told MTV News back in 2010, "Hopefully next summer I can start on a movie or something. [I want] to do a comedy with Will Ferrell, like play his son or something like that." It didn't happen in 2011, but you never know what the future will bring!

Sean Kingston— True Blue Friend

Justin and Sean became close when they collaborated on the single "Eenie Meenie," and that friendship remains strong to this day. Justin proved how much he cared when Sean had a serious jet ski accident in 2011. Justin was one of the first to be there for him, and even stuck around during his recuperation. On an MTV special, Justin did a shout-out to Sean—"I just wanna say what's up Sean, I'm glad you're doing well. I had fun hanging out with you in Miami, and there's plenty more memories to come."

As reported by starpulse.com, Sean replied with love. "That's my lil' bro man... I see that he's a loyal friend. For me to be in a life or death situation like that and then for me to come out the hospital and know that he's calling my mom, calling my manager, calling everybody asking how I'm doing, I see that he's a great friend—a great, true person at heart."

Sean and Justin celebrate the hip-hop star's recovery from a jet ski accident.

Usher Advises Justin

As Justin's mentor and friend, Usher has been there for advice, encouragement, and support. He's had a ton of experience as a solo artist and music producer, and wants to share those lessons with his little bro. "Justin wants everything to be perfect," Usher said in the *2012 Billboard Music Awards Special*. "When his voice was changing, he was really hard on himself; I saw similarities in how when I was his age—I lost my voice completely and had to fight my way back through it. At the time I told him, 'Yo, man, what's the worst that can happen? You go out there and hit a bad note? Make it a part of the show.' After having a career that's spanned as long as mine, I've learned that it's great to be in a moment. That's the coolest part. The more you live in the moment, the greater it is for the moment."

Usher and Justin at Scooter's 30th birthday party.

Mark Wahlberg Shoots Hoops With Justin

During an MTV News interview actor, director, producer, and former rapper Mark Wahlberg talked about a basketball-themed movie he wants to do with Justin. "It's set in [the world of] street-hustling basketball," Wahlberg explained. "Obviously, [Bieber] is a very good athlete. People have seen him on MTV; he can play. But I also really think he can act. . . . There's not going to be any shortage of pushing him in getting that kind of strong performance out of him, if we get to make the movie." Then he jokingly added, "We're just going to have to make him realize that he's playing a character so he can't have the same hairdo."

Later, when Justin was also on MTV, he said, "I'm still working on this movie with Mark Wahlberg. I don't know what the deal is. Turns out they're rewriting the script or something, trying to make it fit better and stuff. It's really cool. Hopefully, I'll be able to do that as well soon. So, I'll be hooping. I got to get back in the gym. I haven't played basketball in a while. I did like a little charity basketball game at Shaq's house for Pencils of Promise. We did a little charity basketball game, and I won."

Mark Wahlberg and JB will be teaming up to make a basketball movie. Mark believes that Justin has the moves both on the court and on screen!

Justin joins Jaden and Willow Smith on stage.

Jaden Smith & Justin . . . Partners in Pranks

Friends since Justin recorded "Never Say Never" for Jaden's *The Karate Kid* soundtrack, the two haven't stopped laughing together since! They love pranking each other, but sometimes they pull in someone else to face the music. Take, for example, a particular incident when Jaden's sister, Willow Smith, was on tour with Justin in 2011. They were in Manchester, England, and Willow was on stage singing her hit, "Whip My Hair." The Justin/Jaden prank started with Justin's manager, Scooter Braun, and "swagger coach," Ryan Good donning Willow's signature neon braids and make-up and taking to the stage as back-up dancers. Next, Jayden and Justin, who was clanging a cowbell, joined them. It was utter chaos. Later, Justin posted on his Facebook page, "MANCHESTER was INCREDIBLE tonight...one of my favorite shows ever!! Pranked Willow during WhipMyHair and then got crazy during the show."

But Willow promised she would have the last laugh. She tweeted, "My big brothers Justin and Jaden pranked me on stage tonight . . . #payback!!!"

Ashton Kutcher & Justin . . . House Flipping

Justin and Ashton are both big fans of pranking their friends. In the spring of 2012, Justin followed Ashton's lead by appearing on MTV's *Punk'd*, where he put Taylor Swift through a mini-trauma. When the teen star began shopping for a house in the L.A. area, his first pick was an estate in the Hollywood Hills. Problem was, Ashton had just rented it.

The two discussed the "standoff" when they were on *Jimmy Kimmel Live!* in March. "I had to buy the house because I thought he was going to buy it out from under me," Ashton told Kimmel. "I was like 'I don't want to lose this house'. He forced me to buy a house. He's trying to steal my swagger."

Ashton explained he had been looking for a place in L.A. for a number of months. "I knew I had to come back and do *Two and a Half Men* in January, so I found this amazing house in L.A. . . . and I booked this house to stay in for three months. I was away, I booked the house, it was all done. . . . All of a sudden my assistant tells me there's somebody coming to look at the house to maybe buy it."

Pointing at Justin, Ashton continued, "I get a text from this guy and he's in my house, checking it out, trying to buy my house. . . . He's like 'Yo, I'm in your house right now. I'm checking it out.' I'm like 'What? Are you trying to take my house from under me?'"

Ashton quickly made the real estate deal, and Justin moved on and then moved into his new digs in Calabasas!

Ashton Kutcher and Justin joke it up on Jimmy Kimmel Live!

Ryan Seacrest & Justin

Justin and TV host, D.J., and producer Ryan Seacrest are good buds. Whenever Justin has an announcement, one of his first stops is 102.7 KIIS-FM's *On-Air With Ryan Seacrest*.

Scooter Braun

Scott "Scooter" Braun's story of discovering a young Justin Bieber is the stuff of legend, and the bond they share to this day is equally unconventional. Justin values Scooter as a manager and as a friend. He has trusted this 31-year-old talent manager to guide him through the ups and downs of a very tricky business, and has appreciated his wise advice. Today, Justin is one of the most successful celebrities around. *Forbes,* a financial magazine, named him the third Most Powerful Celebrity of 2012. But Justin is the first to say that he would never have achieved any of this superstardom without Scooter. From signing with L.A. Reid and Island Def Jam Records to recommending such social media assets as Spotify as promotional tools and investments, Scooter has never steered Justin in the wrong direction. "Spotify was something that I got involved with really early," Justin told *Billboard.* "My manager Scooter talked to me about it from the beginning and I thought it was a good tool because you get almost every song ever made on there and you can buy it whenever you want. I invested mainly because I liked the product."

But that's only the professional side of their relationship. Justin and Scooter are true friends who respect each other, and Scooter just beams when he talks about the rise of Justin from kid to SUPERSTAR. "He was literally going through puberty in front of the entire world, with everyone expecting something from him and a lot of people waiting for him to screw up," Scooter told *Billboard.* "He's a fighter. I'm proud of him—how he's stayed true to himself and taken control of the entire situation."

Boys' night out for Justin, Scooter, and Usher. The guys came together to honor Jan Smith, Justin's vocal coach, at the 33rd annual Georgia Music Hall of Fame.

Justin and Scooter hit the fashion scene in NYC. They attended the September 2011 Fashion Week event at the Dolce & Gabbana Soho store. Justin's not the only one with swag!

Scooter's Early Advice to Justin

"This is going to happen, Justin. The only thing that can stop you is you. People who fail in this business—the really talented people, I mean—it's never about the music. It's about their personal lives. Stay focused and never mind … [what] anybody says. That's not you, that's them. That's the negative place they want to live in. You choose to live in a positive place." (*Justin Bieber: First Step 2 Forever*)

At the 2012 Tribeca Disruptive Innovation Awards, Scooter and Justin hold their Silver Hammers, given to individuals whose "ideas have broken the mold to create significant impact on the future of our world."

"It's just really exciting. Nothing makes [Justin] happier than being onstage. So it's gonna be fun to get back onto the road. I think he was an amazing performer before, but his level of dance and musicianship and his range [has grown]. He's a veteran now." (Scooter to *MTV News*, June 2012)

CRUISIN' WITH JUSTIN

Justin is already known as a mega car buff. In a few short years, he has collected a small fleet of cars, including a black Mercedes-Benz Sprinter van, a black Smart Car, a chrome electric Fisker Karma, a matte black Range Rover, and a black Batman-themed Cadillac CTS-V coupe. To personalize his rides, Justin has become a frequent visitor at West Coast Customs, home of the artists who individualize all kinds of cars. These masters of customizing have worked on almost all of Justin's cars—both inside and out. Justin definitely has some superstar rides to go along with his Superstar status!

Justin's best-known car has to be his Fisker Karma—an eco-friendly electric car that looks like a ride from the future. This particular dream was an 18th birthday present from Justin's manager Scooter Braun, who presented it to Justin on *The Ellen DeGeneres Show*. "You work really, really hard and I always yell at you, 'Don't get anything flashy. We're not about that. Be humble.' And I kind of broke my own rule. We wanted to make sure, since you love cars, that when you're on the road you are always looking environmentally friendly," Scooter told Justin. "And we decided to get you a car that would make you stand out. I think you know where I'm going, and you're kind of freaking out right now. That's a Fisker Karma."

The 2012 Fisker Karma is one of the most environmentally friendly cars on the road. A perfect 18th birthday present for Justin!

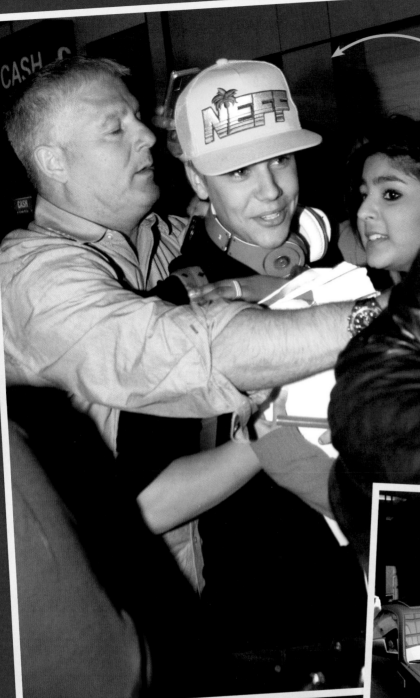

During his London promo-visit, Justin found himself squashed by security guards and fans alike! Bet Justin was thinking, "I'd love to be driving my Fisker Karma right now!"

Justin's Cadillac "Batmobile." Wonder if he feels like a superhero when he's behind the wheel.

Custom Bieber

★ Justin added a chrome wrap, fuchsia LED lights and 22-inch wheels to his Fisker Karma.

★ The regular emblem on the back of his Smart Car was replaced with one that says "Swag Car."

★ Justin's Cadillac CTS-V coupe has a Batman logo on the grill, the word "Batmobile" on the back and Justin's initials on the side panel.

JUSTIN MICS UP!

Can you imagine what it would be like if every time you met someone new, they shoved a microphone in front of your face and asked you dozens of questions? "What made you decide you wanted to join the basketball team at your school?" "Who are your best friends?" "Are you in love?" "What is your favorite subject in school?" And on and on and on.

Well, that's what Justin Bieber deals with every day of his life. If he's not being bombarded by paparazzi with their cameras and questions, he's probably on his way to a press conference with reporters or going to a radio station for a DJ rap with the likes of Ryan Seacrest or Elvis Duran, or visiting one of TV's top talk shows—*Late Show with David Letterman, Jimmy Kimmel Live, The Tonight Show with Jay Leno, The View, The Ellen DeGeneres Show, Late Night with Jimmy Fallon*, BET's *106 & Park*. Over the years, Justin has actually become good buds with some of the hosts—for example, Ryan Seacrest and Jimmy Fallon are definitely guys Justin loves to hang out with. And during his time "on the couch" or "in front of the mic," the cutey from Canada has become pretty comfortable with the patter and chatter. But you never know—sometimes he makes news with a comment or prank. Once he appeared on Jimmy Kimmel's show and "allowed" the host to shave his head—he was wearing a bald cap! And, of course, we know that Justin often uses Ellen DeGeneres's show for major hallmarks, like his birthday, or announcements, like *Believe*'s world tour dates. You just never know what's going to happen!

Justin Gets SiriusXM

Fans, fans everywhere! When Justin hit the SiriusXM studios to promote *Believe*, he was in his usual "let's have fun" mood. After performing in the studio, he took time to chat with fans and sign autographs.

Justin & Jay

In the past, when Justin has been on *The Tonight Show with Jay Leno* he's talked about his super date with Selena for which he rented out the L.A. Staple's Center for dinner and a screening of *Titanic*, discussed his traffic ticket in 2011, and even succeeded in getting Jay to try sushi for the first time! When Justin appeared on the show in June to promote *Believe*, he performed an outrageous version of "Boyfriend," but made big headlines after the show, when he and guitarist/musical director Dan Kanter gave an impromptu acoustic performance for fans in the parking lot of Jay Leno's studio!

Justin & Elvis

On the *Elvis Duran and the Morning Show* in June, not only was Justin excited about the incredible success *Believe* had attained in just a matter of days, he was ecstatic about his performance at the Apollo Theater. "The Apollo was the first place where Michael [Jackson] felt he got his start," Justin told Elvis. "That's what I heard, at least. They drove down as a family and his dad said if you can make it at the Apollo, you can make it anywhere." Also on this visit to Elvis Duran, Justin got to meet an up-and-coming singer, Austin Mahone, who is being dubbed, "Baby Bieber." The hot new singer was thrilled to meet his idol, Mr. Justin Bieber!

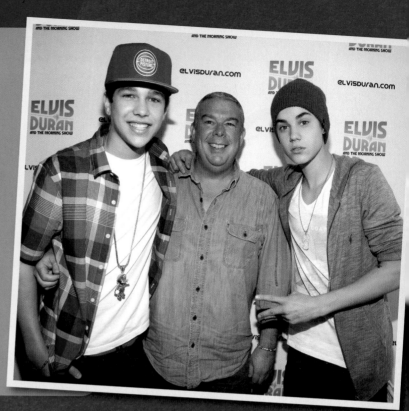

Justin and Rocsi & Terrence

Justin is a regular visitor to BET's *106 & Park*. On his June stop to promote *Believe*, the singer told co-hosts Terrence J and Rosci that he thinks his new CD is going to make people accept that he's growing up, that "now people are judging me for my music." He also said that his favorite song from *Believe* is "Catching Feelings" and "As Long As You Love Me" is the most fun to perform. And where is he most looking forward to traveling to? Japan! Justin loves "the fashion and the culture."

Justin & David

During Justin's June visit to the *Late Show with David Letterman*, the host seemed to put on his "old-guy" hat. Justin was proud to show off his new ink, a tattoo of BELIEVE on his inner left arm. Letterman grumped, "Oh God, how many [tattoos] do you have?" When Justin responded, "a couple," the late night host said, "Tell me that's the last one … Honestly, how does that help you look?" Then he grabbed Justin's arm. Justin jumped back because the tat was brand new and it probably hurt a bit—"Get that off there!" he said. Later Justin dubbed Letterman "Grandpa" for his fuddy-duddy reaction. No more "Uncle Dave!" Wonder what Letterman's reaction will be to Justin's newest ink, which is a small Japanese Kanji symbol for music on the inside of his right forearm?

Justin & Matt

At the *Today* show in June, JB chatted with Matt Lauer and delighted fans with a morning concert. Then he helped launch a whole new phase of the morning show host's career—by introducing him to Twitter. While it's old school for Justin's fans, Lauer had just joined Twitter and asked Justin to help him compose his first Tweet. As Lauer tried to compose a 140-character message, Justin took over and tweeted, "Hello. Everyone go buy Justin Bieber's album #believe coming out June 19th." Justin asked his fans to follow Lauer that day—according to mashable.com, he had more than 100,000 followers in less than 12 hours!

BIEBER BY THE NUMBERS

Justin Bieber has been blessed with big numbers. He has millions of fans and Twitter followers. And his YouTube views, Viddy views, record, concert, and movie box-office sales are proof positive of a devoted Belieber fan-base, almost four years after Bieber Fever first hit the planet.

Twitter Followers: More than 25 million

YouTube Views: More than 2.7 billion

My World Tour: Made more than $50 million

Worldwide CD Sales: 15 million as of May 2012

Most YouTube Views On Debut Day: "Boyfriend"—8 million (100 million as of July 2012 and growing)

Facebook Fans: More than 45 million

Believe Tour

125 concerts

45 North American dates sold out in one hour

Forbes magazine named Justin the third Most Powerful Celebrity in the World in 2012

Justin Bieber: Never Say Never: The 2011 documentary made $98.4 million in theatrical tickets

Instruments: Justin plays four instruments: drums, guitar, piano and trumpet

Justin flashes the peace sign when he leaves the Late Show with David Letterman in June.

Albums that Debuted at Number One

My World 2.0 (2010) sold 283,000 copies the first week

Never Say Never: The Remixes (2011) sold 161,000 copies in the first week

Under The Mistletoe (2011) sold 210,000 copies in the first week

Believe (2012) sold 374,000 copies in the first week

Justin Bieber: First Step 2 Forever: My Story: Was on the *New York Times* Children's Chapter Books Best Seller List for 18 weeks. It was the 9th best-selling children's hardcover book for 2010

Pencils of Promise: One dollar from each ticket of Justin's *Believe* tour will be donated to the charity

NBA All-Star Celebrity Game: Justin scored eight points, four assists and two rebounds in the 2011 basketball game and he won the MVP title for his efforts

Someday: His first perfume made more than $60 million in sales in the first six months when it was introduced in 2011

Madison Square Garden 2012 concerts—November 28th and 29th—sold out in 30 seconds

Forbes magazine named Justin number one on its 2011 list of Celebrity 100 Newcomers

The big number in Justin's life right now is 18! On his birthday, he celebrated with a special "record player" cake when he was interviewed by Z-100's Elvis Duran.

LITTLE-KNOWN BIEBER FACTS

Attention, all you Beliebers! Justin reveals some fun-tastic facts and experiences that may not have made it into the tabloids, teen magazines, or even surfaced on the internet.

Did You Know . . .

Justin is left-handed, but he learned to play on a right-handed guitar. "Because that was all my mom had," he told ABC's *Nightline*. "I picked it up left-handed. My mom would switch it the other way. And I would switch it right back to the other way and try to play. It was difficult, because it's backwards. My mom, I think it was for my birthday, she bought me a left-handed guitar."

Did You Know . . .

Toy company The Bridge Direct made Justin Bieber dolls, and they were just about to hit the store shelves when the singer changed his signature style—he cut his hair! "First off, I had no idea what he did," Bridge Direct CEO Jay Foreman told *Toy News*. "I heard a lot of shrieks around me, and people running in and out of their offices. I got everyone into a conference room and we looked at some images. We weren't sure what he had done. Then it became obvious that his trademark was gone." They ended up spending $100,000 to change the dolls' hair to fit Justin's new look!

Justin held a press conference in Mexico City before performing at a free concert for 200,000 excited fans.

Did You Know . . .

Justin was just about to take a job working at a Stratford fast food restaurant before his career exploded. "I actually applied to A&W before everything happened and then I got a call from my boy Scooter . . ." Justin revealed to NYC Hot 97's DJ Angie Martinez.

Did You Know . . .

Justin almost quit music! "There were so many times when I just wanted to say, 'Enough is enough, I don't want to do this any more,'" Justin told the *Hollywood Reporter*. "I think it's so important to me because it's about my fans and how much they've helped me. They really have kept my heart from falling because they've always been there and supported me and cheered me on."

Did You Know . . .

Justin has taken up a new sport—golf! He's been making good use of the Calabasas Country Club near his new house. Of course, there are times Justin wishes he could have a little more privacy when he's on the links. Once, when he was trying to get a game in, the paparazzi were hiding in the trees trying to get shots of him. He tweeted them, "Dear paps, golf is supposed to be a relaxing sport. U aren't supposed to be in the bushes yelling at me with cameras. Let me finish the game."

Did You Know . . .

Justin wants to go glamping! Glamping—glamorous camping— means going out into the woods to enjoy nature, but with all the luxuries of home. "You sleep on a bed," Justin explained on 102.7 KIIS-FM *On The Air With Ryan Seacrest*. "It's a mattress bed! In a huge tent with a TV and everything. You have electricity and stuff, but you're still in amongst the wildlife. It's pretty cool." He also hinted that he would love to take Selena on a glamping trip!

Did You Know . . .

Justin wasn't always so thrilled about schoolwork, but his tutor, Jenny, knew how to get him to study—and Justin knew how to keep her on her toes. He pranked her at least once a month. He remembers one April Fools' Day in particular in his autobiography *Justin Bieber: First Step 2 Forever*.

"I said to her, 'Hey, Jenny, let's do a science experiment.

'Great idea,' she said, 'Let's do it.'

'I read that if you put salt on top of butter, it heats it up. You can actually feel it.'

'Really? I've never heard that.'

I carefully put a stick of butter on a plate and measured a tablespoon of salt over it.

'Okay, now we have to wait sixty seconds,' I meticulously timed the sixty seconds, then held my hand over the butter. 'Oh, that's wild. You can really feel it. That's amazing. Check it out.'

Jenny held her palm over the plate of butter, and faster than she could react, I pushed her hand down and squished the butter all over.

She was hysterical.

Pranks vs. school=pranks win all day. Can you blame me? I'm just a kid."

THAT HAIR!

When Justin first appeared on the scene in 2009, it wasn't only his angelic voice and face that wowed audiences—his hair was also a major asset! Within weeks, girls were asking their boyfriends to get the trademark "Bieber swoop." The style was probably the most-copied cut since Jennifer Aniston appeared on the TV series *Friends*.

In 2011, just before *Never Say Never* was released, he said to MTV News, "I think after my movie I might cut my hair a little shorter." You would have thought the Earth had stopped turning on its axis! Fans were tweeting Justin, begging him not to change his hair. But when Justin did start experimenting with his hairstyle, his fans embraced the change and have yet to protest any of his new looks. Many guys have continued to use Justin as their hair inspiration—his new, swept-up look seems to have caught on. That Justin. . . always a trend setter!

2009: Justin's famous swoop.

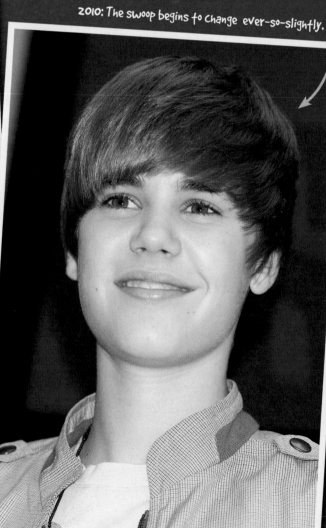

2010: The swoop begins to change ever-so-slightly.

2011: Justin's hair gets a little more styled.

On changing his hair style: "I just wanna be able to rock anything and not really care—whether it's long or short, buzzed, or waxed over. I'm not just going to be known for my hair."—Justin (Seventeen)

2011: Justin's do gets gelled!

103

2011: More product!

2011: Hey, Justin can still do a variation of the swoop!

2012: Justin's new red-carpet look.

2012: A blonder, James Dean-inspired slicked-up look.

WELCOME TO JUSTIN'S OPEN HOUSE

WOW! Justin's first house is anything but a fixer-upper! This gated 10,000-square-foot mansion, located in the beautiful Calabasas area of California, features 1.3 acres, seven bedrooms, eight bathrooms, an outdoor pool, sauna, health spa, a wine cellar, a library, a private screening room, a multi-car garage, and a guesthouse off the pool. Set in the San Fernando Valley, Calabasas is 22 miles from Hollywood, so Justin is totally within driving distance from red carpet events and studio time.

Several weeks before Justin signed the papers to buy his dream house, it was reported that he was eyeing another house in the Hollywood Hills. Unfortunately, his bud Ashton Kutcher had been renting that house, and when he heard that Justin was going to buy it out from under him, he snatched it back. No problem—Calabasas was calling and Justin heard the tune!

Justin bought the house shortly before he started out on his promo-jaunt, the *All Around the World* tour, so he didn't really have much time to buy furniture and settle in. Since then, he has hired a decorator and is reportedly making plans to have a computer system installed that will control every part of the property.

If you believe what he revealed in a June interview with New York City's Hot 97 DJ Angie Martinez, you know he is definitely comfortable in his new digs. "I am running around naked in the house," Biebs told Angie. "That's what you have to do when you—I mean when you get your own place. You feel comfortable to just run around, get some cereal—butt naked!"

Quickies

★ Neighbors include the Kardashians, Cameron Diaz, Lady Gaga, fellow Canadian Drake, Blink-182 drummer Travis Barker, Romeo, NFL player Keyshawn Johnson, and Howie Mandel.

★ Rumor has it that Justin plans on installing a game room with console games and arcade machines.

CONGRATULATIONS!

It's lucky that Justin bought such a big house in Calabasas, California... now he can dedicate an entire room to his awards! In two short years, Justin has accumulated quite a variety—four American Music Awards, seven *Billboard* Music Awards, one Brit Award, one CMT Award, one Georgia Music Hall of Fame award, three Juno Awards, five *J-14* Teen Icon Awards, four MTV Europe Music Awards, one MTV Movie Award, two MTV Music Video Awards, seven MuchMusic Video Awards, one NBA All-Star Celebrity Game Award, two NJR Awards, three Nickelodeon Kids' Choice Awards, one O Music Award, one Starshine Music Award, eight Teen Choice Awards, one Young Hollywood Award, and one FiFi Award—and this isn't even counting the nominations he has received!

It couldn't have been a better night! Not only did Justin perform, but he also won Canada's MuchMusic "UR Fave Artist" Award! "I want to thank the fans. With this album, I was inspired by my fans and they helped me get through a lot," Justin said when accepting the award. "I wrote a song about them and it's called 'Believe.' I can't wait for them to hear it. . . Canada, I will always support you and always love you. It's always great to pull one of these bad boys home."

Oops!

It can get crazy backstage! When Justin headed offstage at the MuchMusic Video Awards, he was swarmed by well-wishers. Thinking that he was handing his "UR Fave Artist" trophy to one of the awards representatives, he passed it on, but the recipient was actually a fan! When the MuchMusic officials tracked her down, she kindly gave it back to them. Wonder if she included a note to Justin. . .

Justin won the 2012 Favorite Male Singer trophy blimp at the Nickelodeon Kids' Choice Awards. He had just shot his video for "Boyfriend," and obviously had his upcoming album on his mind. "Right now, I've been working really hard on my album, Believe. This album is our album. This [blimp] goes out to all the fans. I love you so much," he said to the Kids' Choice audience.

Justin accepted the 2012 Tribeca Disruptive Innovation Award, along with Scooter Braun. They were chosen for their unique and successful use of social media in building Justin's music career.

Justin brought the *Billboard* Music Awards audience to its feet when he performed "Boyfriend." The room shook again when he was given the "Top Social Artist" award.

It was pandemonium on June 19th in downtown New York City! Justin arrived at the J&R Music World store to sign autographs and promote his new album, *Believe*. Fans had lined up for hours just to get a glimpse of their "Boyfriend." While he was there, Justin was honored with a proclamation from the City of New York that deemed June 19th "Justin Bieber J&R Appreciation Day."

Justin made a surprise appearance at the 2011 MTV Movie Awards to accept the golden popcorn trophy for "Best Jaw Dropping Moment" for *Justin Bieber: Never Say Never 3D*. He thanked his director, his manager, and family, and added, "but most of all I want to thank my fans. I love you."

BIEBER FAMILY FUN QUIZ

Test your knowledge of all things Bieber family and Canadian roots! Justin often talks about his early days and how the love and support of his mom, dad, grandparents, and friends helped him face some tough times. It is his family's unfailing love and support that helps him keep his feet on the ground and head out of the clouds. You'll need to be a true Belieber to know some of these answers. Not all of the answers are in this book.

FILL IN THE BLANKS

1 Justin and his grandfather like going fishing on

2 When Justin was little, his dad worked in

3 Justin's favorite NHL team is the

4 Justin's mom, Pattie, used to play this group's albums all the time

5 The name of the singing competition that started it all for Justin is

Dad Jeremy carried little Jazmyn into the hotel in Madrid when they visited Justin during his *All Around the World* tour.

TRUE OR FALSE

Having his little sister with him during the Madrid leg of his *All Around The World* tour made Justin very happy. What is her name?

1

Justin and his mom Pattie struggled to make ends meet when he was growing up.

TRUE or FALSE?

2

Justin hates pizza with pineapple topping.

TRUE or FALSE?

3

Justin loved playing badminton, squash, and water polo when he was growing up.

TRUE or FALSE?

4

The Stratford restaurant, King's Buffet, was the site of Justin's first date.

TRUE or FALSE?

5

Justin's first instrument was the drums.

TRUE or FALSE?

Back home in Canada, Justin lets his hair down and just chills.

TRUE OR FALSE ANSWERS: 1) True —he has said they lived below the poverty level; 2)False—he loves pineapple pizza; 3) False—his sports were soccer, hockey, and basketball; 4) True—he says it didn't go so well; 5) True—it was a full, professional set

FILL IN THE BLANKS ANSWERS: 1) Star Lake; 2) Construction; 3) Maple Leafs; 4) Boyz II Men; 5) the Stratford Star competition

MULTIPLE CHOICE

1 Justin's maternal grandparents are:
- **A)** Barry and Debby
- **B)** Bruce and Diane
- **C)** Bobby and Deena

2 Justin's mom's name is:
- **A)** Pattie Mallette
- **B)** Patricia Maller
- **C)** Patty Mahone

3 Justin is originally from this town in Ontario, Canada:
- **A)** Halton Hill
- **B)** Cambridge
- **C)** Stratford

4 Justin's father's name is Jeremy Bieber. His middle name is:
- **A)** Jesse
- **B)** James
- **C)** Jack

5 Justin's half brother and sister's names are:
- **A)** Jesse and Jessica
- **B)** Jaxon and Jazmyn
- **C)** Johnny and Joyce

6 The name of the theater that Justin busked in front of is:
- **A)** Avon Theatre
- **B)** Aria Theatre
- **C)** Austin Theatre

7 Justin can speak this language:
- **A)** German
- **B)** Japanese
- **C)** French

8 Justin's middle name is:
- **A)** Dennis
- **B)** Drew
- **C)** Damon

9 Justin's hometown is on the banks of this river:
- **A)** The Avon River
- **B)** The Hudson River
- **C)** The Blue River

10 Justin's best friends from home are:
- **A)** Ryan and Chaz
- **B)** Roger and Chris
- **C)** Ray and Carmine

ANSWERS: 1) b; 2) a; 3) c; 4) b; 5) b; 6) a; 7) c; 8) b; 9) a; 10) a.

Justin arrives at the Entertainment Quarter for his acoustic concert in Sydney, Australia, July 17, 2012.

JUSTIN'S SING-ALONG WORD SCRAMBLE

Bet you know all the lyrics to his songs! After all, you are a big Belieber, right? Well, now it's time to be a Belieber Brainiac and solve these word scrambles based on Justin's song titles. The tracks come from his four albums, *My World 2.0*, *Never Say Never: The Remixes*, *Under The Mistletoe*, and *Believe*. Some are easy, and some are more difficult, so we may just give you a hint here and there. Start scrambling!

Justin sings his heart out, crooning some of his dreamy lyrics.

1 YABB

This one is too easy to give you a hint!

2 ROBN OT EB YEDMOOSB

It's from the *Never Say Never—The Remixes* album

3 EEEIN NEEMIE

Sean Kingston collaborated with Justin on this one

4 LAL I NATW ORF SAMTSIRHC SI YOU

This was a duet with Nick Cannon's wife

5 SA NGOL SA UoY EoLV EM

Big Sean jammed with Justin on this one

6 U ELSMI

This was the third single from Justin's *My World 2.0* album

7 LAL NDUoRA HET DLWoR

Ludacris joins Justin on this song

8 ENVER YAS ENVER

This was on the soundtrack for *The Karate Kid*

9 EID NI OURY MARS

This was released in the spring of 2012

10 OYFRBEIDN

Every girl wishes Justin was hers

ANSWERS: 1) "Baby"; 2) "Born To Be Somebody"; 3) "Eenie Meenie"; 4) "All I Want For Christmas Is You"; 5) "As Long As You Love Me"; 6) "U Smile"; 7) "All Around The World"; 8) "Never Say Never"; 9) "Die In Your Arms"; 10) "Boyfriend".

R U A JB WIZ KID?

Trivia, trivia, trivia! On the following pages is Bieber-trivia galore. Some of these fun facts you'll already know, and others may surprise you.

How It All Started—First Six JB YouTube Videos (Kidrauhl Site)

1) Justin singing "So Sick" by Ne-Yo

2) Snippet of Justin on someone's old drums

3) Justin playing "Kate's Song" on the keyboards

4) Justin singing in the bathroom—"Back at One" by Brian McNight

5) Justin Bieber playing the Djembe

6) Justin singing "Set a Place at Your Table," an Original

O Canada!

Though Justin has lost some of his Canadian accent, he hasn't lost any love for his home country. "Canada is an awesome country in general, and Stratford is an excellent place to call home. The people are nice, but not easily impressed." (*Justin Bieber: First Step 2 Forever*)

After the "slime-time" at the 2012 Kids' Choice Awards, Justin chatted with soccer superstar David Beckham's sons (left to right), Romeo, Brooklyn, and Cruz.

Michael Jackson has always been an icon to Justin, so he was thrilled when he got to meet the late singer's family (left to right): son Prince Michael, mother Katherine, son Blanket, and daughter Paris.

Hometown Honor

Since Stratford is one of Canada's most famous arts centers, it isn't surprising that there are bronze stars planted in the sidewalk throughout the downtown streets. Think Hollywood's Walk of Fame. Justin got his "Bronze Star" on July 1, 2011.

Justin sang "Someday at Christmas" for President Obama at the Christmas in Washington special. Wonder what Justin thinks of the viral video mashup of President Obama singing "Boyfriend"?

Bieber Cares

Justin believes it's his duty to give back, to share with those who aren't as lucky as he is. Here are a few of his favorite charities:

Pencils of Promise: This non-profit organization helps build and supply schools all around the world, especially in emerging nations. (Part of the profits for Justin's fragrances Someday and Girlfriend are donated to them.)

Make-a-Wish Foundation: This organization is the world's largest wish-granting charity. It helps turn dreams into reality for children with life-threatening conditions. (It also recieves a portion of Justin's fragrance profits.)

The *Believe* Charity Drive: On the release of *Under The Mistletoe*, Justin announced that a portion of the album's proceeds would go to seven charitable organizations— the Make-A-Wish Foundation, Pencils of Promise, Musicians on Call, Project Medishare for Haiti, City of Hope, the Boys & Girls Clubs of America and the Grammy Foundation. According to a press release, Justin chose these organizations because of "their emphases on education, youth well-being and music." The drive continues with the release of *Believe*. You can make donations on Justin's official website: justinbiebermusic.com.

Stratford House of Blessing: This is a food bank that helps those in need in Justin's hometown, Stratford, and in other towns nearby. In October 2011, he donated $10,000 to the center. This charity is particularly special to Justin because it helped him and his mom survive some difficult times.

Justin visits the Daily Bread Food Bank in Toronto over the Christmas holidays.

"I am launching the *Believe* Charity Drive because I know firsthand that if you believe in your dreams, everything is possible. The *Believe* Charity Drive directly benefits charities that are making a difference in the world. You can. . . donate as little as one dollar, or even donate your time, because everything will make a difference." (Justin Bieber Press Release)

JB SHOE BIZ QUIZ

Justin is well known for his major collection of kicks—high-tops and sky-tops, running and b-ball shoes, sports and skateboarding gear... Justin's got it all, and in every color of the rainbow! As a Bieber fan, you will probably recognize some of his favorites shoes, but here's the place to put your abilities to the test! Below are six shots of celebrities' unique footwear. Three photos are of Justin, and three photos are of other hotties you know. Your job is to pick out Justin's shoes, and if you're really a celebrity spotter, identify the others too. On your mark, get set, go!

PHOTO OOPS!

"Justin! Look over here!" "Justin! Smile!" "Justin! Justin! Justin!" The paparazzi shouts must echo in Justin's ears. Everyone wants to get that perfect shot: the one that captures the style, the swag, and the charm, that could grace the cover of a magazine. Those shots that do catch Justin looking straight into the camera and smiling brightly are worth a lot, but you might be surprised to know that there are even more sought-after photographs of the teen star: the embarrassing ones! Those photographs of celebrities tripping, sneezing, eating, or having a wardrobe malfunction are definitely attention-grabbing.

Though he may be young, Justin has become a seasoned vet when it comes to these photo ops and photo oops. He's learned to go with the flow . . . and laugh when he's caught not looking so Bieberlicious! Check out some of his funniest photo moments.

"No one is safe from the slime!" yelled Will Smith at the 2012 Nickelodeon Kids' Choice Awards. "You have to earn the slime! It's an honor." And honored, Justin certainly was. When Will presented JB his "Favorite Male Singer" blimp, the entire stage was showered with Nick's famous green goo. It may have been icky, but Justin smiled through it all!

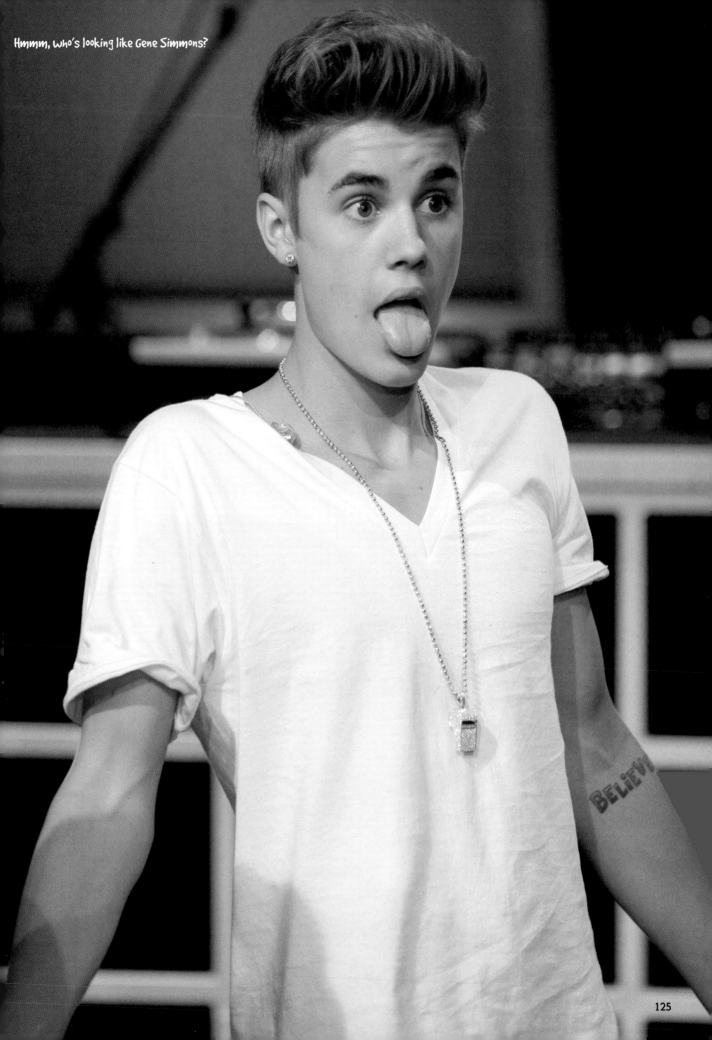

Justin may have been smiling when he posed with rock 'n roll's wild man Ozzy Osbourne for the Best Buy commercial that ran during the 2011 Super Bowl, but the space suit was hardly our favorite look!

While in New York City in 2011, Justin had a craving for a slice of pizza. He and road manager Kenny Hamilton hit Ray's pizza—along with a bunch of fans who must have been really hungry!

During a visit to NYC's Sirius XM radio headquarters, Justin looks like he's got some "Bieber Fever"!

WE'VE GOT BIEBER FEVER

Wonder if Usher knew that Justin was making a funny face behind his back while posing for pics backstage at the 33rd Annual Georgia Music Hall of Fame Awards. . .

Whoops! Justin almost pulled a pants on the ground moment! Maybe he should invest in a better belt. . .

PHOTO CREDITS

Front cover: Gregg DeGuire/WireImage/Getty Images. 2: Josiah Kamau/BuzzFoto/FilmMagic/Getty Images. 6–7: Kristian Dowling/Getty Images. 8: Neil Mockford/FilmMagic/Getty Images. 9: Mark Davis/WireImage/Getty Images. 10: Kevin Winter/Getty Images. 11–12: Ethan Miller/Billboards2012/Getty Images for ABC (all). 13: Victor Chavez/WireImage/Getty Images. 14: Vittorio Zunino Celotto/Getty Images. 15: Rick Diamond/Getty Images for CMT. 16 Will Hart/NBC/NBCU Photo Bank via Getty Images. 17: Paul Drinkwater/NBC/NBCU Photo Bank via Getty Images. 18: Stephen Lovekin/FilmMagic/Getty Images. 19: Kevin Mazur/WireImage/Getty Images. 20: Debra L Rothenberg/FilmMagic/Getty Images. 21: Stephen Lovekin/FilmMagic/Getty Images (point), Kevin Mazur/WireImage/Getty Images (with phone). 22–23: Kevin Mazur/WireImage/Getty Images (all). 24: Jared Milgrim/Getty Images. 25: Neil Mockford/FilmMagic/Getty Images. 26: Lewis Jacobs/NBC/NBCU Photo Bank via Getty Images. 27: Juan Naharro Gimenez/Getty Images. 28–29: Ian Gavan/Getty Images for Universal (all). 30: Vittorio Zunino Celotto/Getty Images. 31: © Splash News/Corbis (all). 32: Luca Teuchmann/Getty Images (mic), Peter Wafzig/Getty Images (walk). 33: Peter Wafzig/Getty Images. 34: Victor Chavez/WireImage/Getty Images. 35: Victor Chavez/WireImage/Getty Images (alone), Ronaldo Schemidt/AFP/Getty Images (dancers). 36–37: George Pimentel/WireImage/Getty Images (all). 38–39: Will Hart/NBC/NBCU Photo Bank via Getty Images (all). 40: Victor Chavez/WireImage/Getty Images. 41: James Devaney/WireImage/Getty Images. 42: Kevin Winter/NBCUniversal/Getty Images (perfume), Roger Kisby/Getty Images (standing). 43: Kevin Mazur/WireImage/Getty Images. 44: Juan Naharro Gimenez/Getty Images. 45: Josiah Kamau/BuzzFoto/Getty Images (sunglasses), Kevin Winter/Getty Images (plaid shirt). 46: Valerie Macon/AFP/Getty Images. 47–48: Kevin Mazur/WireImage/Getty Images (all). 49: © Splash News/Corbis (all). 50–51: Noel Vasquez/Getty Images (all). 52–53: BuzzFoto/BuzzFoto/FilmMagic/Getty Images (all). 54–56: © Splash News/Corbis (all). 57: BuzzFoto/BuzzFoto/FilmMagic/Getty Images. 58: John Lamparski/Getty Images (alone), Dave Benett/MTV 2011/Getty Images (with Perry). 59: Kevin Mazur/TCA 2011/Getty Images (with Swift), Kevin Mazur/WireImage/Getty Images (with Kardashian). 60: Jason Merritt/Getty Images for GLAAD (DeGeneres), Kevin Mazur/WireImage/Getty Images (with Panettiere). 61: Will Hart/NBC/NBCU Photo Bank via Getty Images. 62: Mark Davis/WireImage/Getty Images (with Jepsen), Bill McCay/WireImage/Getty Images (Jepsen). 63: George Pimentel/WireImage/Getty Images. 64: Ben Rose/WireImage/Getty Images. 65: John Lamparski/Getty Images. 66: © Splash News/Corbis. 67: Christopher Polk/Billboards2012/Getty Images for ABC. 68: Jag Gundu/Getty Images. 69: Joe Scarnici/WireImage/Getty Images (with Minaj), Kevin Mazur/WireImage/Getty Images (with Big Sean), Moses Robinson/Getty Images (with Ludacris). 70: Paul Drinkwater/NBC/NBCU Photo Bank via Getty Images. 71: John Paul Filo/CBS via Getty Images (tattoo), Juan Naharro Gimenez/Getty Images (Segway). 72: © Splash News/Corbis (soccer), Michael Buckner/WireImage/Getty Images (slime). 73: © Splash News/Corbis (skateboard), George Pimentel/WireImage/Getty Images (hockey), Riccardo Savi/WireImage/Getty Images (hospital). 74–75: George Pimentel/WireImage/Getty Images (all). 76: George Pimentel/WireImage/Getty Images (sister), Stephen Lovekin/Getty Images (mom). 77: Gareth Cattermole/Getty Images. 78: ChinaFotoPress/ChinaFotoPress/Getty Images. 79: © Splash News/Corbis. 80: Steve Mack/FilmMagic/Getty Images. 81: Peter Kramer/NBC/NBC NewsWire via Getty Images. 82: Christopher Peterson/BuzzFoto/FilmMagic/Getty Images. 83–84: George Pimentel/WireImage/Getty Images (all). 84: Kevin Winter/Getty Images. 85: Europa Press/Europa Press/Getty Images. 86: Kevin Winter/Getty Images (with Simmons), Christopher Polk/Getty Images for VH1 (with Ferrell). 87: Kevin Mazur/TCA 2011/WireImage/Getty Images (with Kingston), Charley Gallay/WireImage/Getty Images (with Usher). 88: Kevork Djansezian/WireImage/Getty Images (Wahlberg), Christopher Polk/KCA2012/Getty Images for KCA (with Smiths). 89: Randy Holmes/Disney ABC Television Group/Getty Images (with Kutcher), Michael Kovac/Getty Images (Seacrest). 90: Ben Rose/WireImage/Getty Images (with Braun and Usher), Stephen Lovekin/Getty Images (with Braun). 91: Dimitrios Kambouris/WireImage/Getty Images. 92: © Ciao Hollywood /Splash News/Corbis. 93: Alex Moss/FilmMagic/Getty Images (Justin), © Splash News/Corbis (Cadillac). 94: Roger Kisby/Getty Images. 95: Paul Drinkwater/NBC/NBCU Photo Bank via Getty Images. 96: Kevin Mazur/WireImage/Getty Images (z100), D Dipasupil/Getty Images (106 & Park). 97: John Paul Filo/CBS via Getty Images (alone), Peter Kramer/NBC/NBC NewsWire via Getty Images (Today). 98: James Devaney/WireImage/Getty Images. 99: Kevin Winter/Getty Images. 100: Clasos/CON/LatinContent Editorial/Getty Images. 101: Kristian Dowling/Getty Images (Justin), Torbjorn Lagerwall/Photos.com (butter). 102: Mike Coppola/FilmMagic/Getty Images (left), Jun Sato/WireImage/Getty Images (right). 103: Steve Granitz/WireImage/Getty Images (left), Jordan Strauss/WireImage/Getty Images (right). 104: Dave J Hogan/Getty Images (left), Gary Gershoff/WireImage/Getty Images (right). 105: Pascal Le Segretain/Getty Images (left), George Pimentel/WireImage/Getty Images (right). 106: © Splash News/Corbis. 107: John Lamparski/Getty Images. 108: Sonia Recchia/WireImage/Getty Images. 109: Kevork Djansezian/Getty Images. 110: Dimitrios Kambouris/WireImage/Getty Images (hammer), Ethan Miller/Billboards2012/Getty Images for ABC (award). 111: Jamie McCarthy/WireImage/Getty Images (proclamation), Kevin Mazur/WireImage/Getty Images (popcorn). 112: Europa Press/Europa Press/Getty Images. 113: Europa Press/Europa Press/Getty Images (sister), © Splash News/Corbis (soccer). 114: George Pimentel/WireImage/Getty Images. 115: Caroline McCredie/Getty Images. 116: Will Hart/NBC/NBCU Photo Bank via Getty Images. 117: Victor Chavez/WireImage/Getty Images. 118: Charley Gallay/KCA2012/Getty Images. 119: Josiah Kamau/BuzzFoto/FilmMagic/Getty Images. 120: Lester Cohen/WireImage/Getty Images (with Jacksons), Larry Busacca/WireImage/Getty Images (with Obama). 121: George Pimentel/WireImage/Getty Images. 122: Jon Kopaloff/FilmMagic/Getty Images (1), Jason Merritt/Getty Images (2). 123: Jason LaVeris/FilmMagic/Getty Images(3, 5), Amanda Edwards/Getty Images (4), Jon Kopaloff/FilmMagic/Getty Images (6). 124: Kevork Djansezian/Getty Images (all). 125: Paul Drinkwater/NBC/NBCU Photo Bank via Getty Images. 126: Christopher Polk/Getty Images for Best Buy (with Osbourne), James Devaney/WireImage/Getty Images (glasses), Roger Kisby/Getty Images (fever). 127: Ben Rose/WireImage/Getty Images (with Usher), Kevin Winter/Getty Images (pants). Back cover: Paul Drinkwater/NBC/NBCU Photo Bank via Getty Images (top left), Christopher Polk/Billboards2012/Getty Images for ABC (top center), Josiah Kamau/BuzzFoto/FilmMagic/Getty Images (top right), BuzzFoto/BuzzFoto/FilmMagic/Getty Images (bottom left), Vittorio Zunino Celotto/Getty Images (bottom right).